We're Loyal to You, Gilman High

We're Loyal to You, Gilman High

Story of a High School Basketball Player

by Benjamin Herrold

ISBN 978-1-58597-450-4
Library of Congress Control Number: 2007940994

4500 College Boulevard
Overland Park, Kansas 66211
888-888-7696
www.leatherspublishing.com

CHAPTER 1

Gilman City is a small town. Many people talk about "quiet villages" and "sleepy little towns" of a few thousand people. Gilman (most locals don't bother to say the city part) has city limit signs that boast a population of 380. When buying a road atlas, Gilman City is my barometer of how detailed the state maps are. Detailed maps show a black dot representing the town at the juncture of State Highway 146 and State Highway K, while less diligent editions omit the town. This is the town in which I would play my high school basketball career.

Gilman City wasn't always an insignificant little map dot. It was established in 1897 when most of the town of Bancroft moved one mile north to be along the new railroad line. The town was much bigger than it is today and was a busy little railroad town for decades. Somewhere along the way the trains quit coming and the tracks were removed, and Gilman City became purely an agricultural town.

Gilman City sits in northwest Missouri. The area is lightly populated. The town sits at the very southern edge of Harrison County, with the Harrison-Daviess county line road marking the town's southern border.

Towering over the north end of town is the great white water tower. The water tower is to Gilman City as Mt. Rainier is to Seattle.

From anywhere in town, you can see the water tower, standing watch over the town, tall and unchanging.

Main Street runs through the north end of town, known as "uptown." This is the business district with a few restaurants, a lumberyard, a barber shop/pool hall, a park, and the gas station. The iconic "station" is where several older citizens sit amidst cumulus clouds of cigarette smoke and talk about anything and everything. Like many small towns, Gilman City's main street has its share of empty brick buildings.

The school is at the south end of town, a looming brick structure three times as tall as any other building in town, unless you count the grain elevator across the street. It's a sturdy child of the Roaring Twenties, hosting kindergarten through 12th grade all in one building. Technically, there is another building for music and Ag, but almost everything takes place in the main building. Educating grades K-12 in one building seems to be as archaic as the drop kick

Several Businesses line Main Street in uptown Gilman City.
It's a nice friendly little town.

in football, but it works just fine for Gilman City. It's worked for my family; I'm the third generation to go to school there. Connected to the school on the east side is the gym that was added in the late 1950s. The gym, with its big arched roof, replaced the older, smaller gym in the main building.

There is no football field, because Gilman City doesn't have a football team, like many small schools in the area. Instead, the school has a boys' fast pitch softball team that plays in the fall, one of roughly two dozen in state. Boys and Girls softball are played in the fall, like football. Although boys' fast pitch softball is not yet sanctioned by MSHSAA, there is a state tournament every year in Chillicothe. Gilman won the tournament once in 1993 when current coach Brent Burke was in high school. It is Gilman City's only state championship in any sport. We were also second in the state tournament my freshman year and fourth my senior year.

The softball field lies between the school and the barns that store buses and are used for the Gilman City fair every summer. Overall, the softball field is a pretty nice facility, especially after the outfield fence was installed for my senior season. Before, a well-placed hit to the gap could roll and roll and roll while some poor outfielder would run after it, like a greyhound after a mechanical rabbit. While there are a few little rocks on the infield and the outfield has a few uneven spots, Coach Burke did a good job keeping the playing surface in good shape. Burke is the school's boys basketball coach, boys softball coach, P.E./Health teacher, class sponsor for my class, and softball groundskeeper.

I once got a good view of the school grounds when my class went on the roof of the school to take a senior class picture. The view was stunning. The town sits on a flat area my grandpa always calls the "Blue Ridge prairie." This increased how far I could see. I could see farmland extending for miles in the morning sunlight. It was beautiful. It reminded me of the view from Pike's Peak, looking out over the Great Plains. I could see a car driving away down Highway K. I could watch the tiny speck of the vehicle drive away for miles. Bringing my focus closer to where I was, I could look down on the black, arching roof of the gym.

The gym was one of my favorite places in the school. I spent a lot of time playing basketball there, both in practice and in games. Beyond that, it's where I graduated, where I went to several programs and pep rallies, and where I will be attending alumni banquets for who knows how long. I respect the gym. Playing basketball in the gym gives you a link to many other people in the town. You are a part of history.

The gym has bleacher seats on the north side, elevated so the first row is about five or six feet above the court. I'm well acquainted with this section of the gym after countless sessions of running stairs. The south side of the court is the benches and the stage, on which extra bleachers were assembled for the Gilman City Tournament and Homecoming games. Almost everything in the gym that can be is painted blue. Blue and white with red trim are the school colors. The locker rooms are another story. They're cold, they smell bad, and there's usually wadded-up, used clothes lying around. But locker rooms aren't supposed to be the governor's mansion, are they?

The gym is a historic artifact, a place Gilman Citians have been going for decades, like the station. Except for a cosmetic change or a scoreboard change here or there, the gym is the same as when my dad played there in the 1970s. With its loud crowds, it's also a great home field advantage.

Two blue banners hang on the south walls of the gym. They show the rich tradition of sports at Gilman City by listing every conference title, district title, and state top four finish. It's a subtle reminder to current players what they are a part of.

While all sports have had some success, basketball is the sport at Gilman City. The hoops tradition goes back to the early parts of the century, when Gilman was winning indoor and outdoor county tournaments. Starting in 1928, Gilman City has won 22 boys district titles, including one in every decade since the 1920s. Gilman City girls have won 8 district titles since the current girls' state tournament format was established in the 1970s.

A newspaper once jokingly (I think) reported how Gilman City society worked. When kids reached high school, they were sent to one end of Main Street, where they shot at a hoop. If they made the shot, they played basketball. If they missed the shot, they kept on walking, never to be seen again. It's an exaggeration, but good basketball players have long been valued in Gilman City. Whenever I would tell someone I am from Gilman, the first thing they usually would ask is if I play basketball.

The town's teams have had some success on big stage of the state playoffs. In 1945, Gilman took third in state in an era without class distinctions. Gilman lost to Springfield in the state semifinals that year, but rallied to win the third place game for the school's highest state finish before or since. In 1957 and 1961, Gilman City took 4th in state. In 1994, Gilman narrowly missed its fourth trip to the Final Four in a one-point loss in the state quarterfinal game at Maryville. The closest the Gilman City Lady Hawks have come to a Final Four berth was in 2006. Gilman lost to eventual state champion DeKalb in the quarterfinals that year and finished the year ranked 9th in the final state poll. It was a magical year that included a 17-game winning streak and a miraculous, comeback, overtime win over rival Tri-County in the sectional game at Chillicothe. My younger sister, Abbie, was on that team.

It would be nice to portray Gilman as a friendly little town with great basketball tradition. Unfortunately, there's more to it, as is the case with most towns. Alcohol is a problem in the town. Kids start hitting the booze at alarmingly young ages. Drinking and driving, that dangerous and selfish crime, is mostly accepted among high school kids.

With almost nothing else to do around town, kids go out and get drunk, futilely trying to get away or experience something worthwhile. I would say 90% of the kids in high school drank alcohol when I went to school, but that could be an overly conservative estimate. Also, I was shocked how many kids had tried marijuana by the time I was a senior. I never drank or partied because I had my own standards and God's standards for me that I would not compromise. One of the town's biggest problems seems to be that most high school kids have no moral standards of their own. There is only the community standard, which most kids follow like obedient little Communists. The high school community moral standard is very low, basically saying if it seems fun, do it. Sleep with whomever you want and put anything you feel like in your body. Perhaps the most tragic part of it all is that the kids who drink and party don't know there could be more to life than drinking like a fish and waking up with a headache. I should have been more vocal about how I feel when I was in high school.

For its good and bad, it was in this town and this gym that I would play my basketball career, from elementary basketball to junior high to high school. I became a part of Gilman City's rich basketball tradition. In my high school career, which was three years long, I started and played all 80 games the team played. I scored over 1,000 points and had over 650 rebounds. I tried to be a consistent, team player who displayed good sportsmanship and didn't get rattled no matter what the situation. Overall, I think I did these things, though I certainly wasn't the greatest player to ever come around. My career seemed to have several ups and downs, as I can think of several euphoric victories and crushing losses.

My high school basketball career has left me with vivid memories I'll always remember, such as Homecoming games, tournament championship games, rivalry games, endless (or so I thought) practices, bumpy bus rides to games, playing in all kinds of gyms, and many others, plus all the events of high school life outside of basketball.

It is my hope this story can help readers understand what it was like to go to high school and play basketball in Gilman City, Missouri. It was a unique situation and perhaps my experiences will remind readers of their own days playing high school basketball.

CHAPTER 2

Gilman City sits among several other small towns in north-west Missouri. The area is lightly populated, in the sometimes forgotten part of the state north of US Highway 36. It's in a seemingly endless, nearly empty expanse of rolling hills between Kansas City and Des Moines. Up here the roads are cracked, warped parodies of actual highways. In northwest Missouri, 24-hour gas stations and movie theaters are rare. However, the area is long on open spaces and (usually) friendly people. Northwest Missouri isn't wide open in the desolate way of the Great Plains to the west, but more to a quiet, relaxing degree.

Gilman City is one of 11 schools that make up the HDC Conference. The letters HDC stand for Harrison, Daviess and Caldwell counties, although the conference no longer has any representatives from Caldwell County. Also, teams from Mercer, Grundy, and Sullivan Counties have joined the conference. However, the HDC kept the name everyone knows it by, in the same way that the 11-team Big 10 Conference kept its traditional name.

The schools in the HDC are small. Gilman City averages about 10 students per grade, and it is of average size for the conference. The bigger, county seat towns in the area make up the Grand River Conference. Although all HDC schools are classified as 1A, they often play 2A and 3A schools from the GRC, winning sometimes.

Each HDC team has its own style and reputation. Looking at the HDC schools gives a context for basketball in northwest Missouri.

Probably Gilman City's biggest rival is the Tri-County Mustangs, whose colors are also blue and white. The Tri-County School is located in Jamesport, a town of 507 people. Jamesport is fairly close to Gilman City, and the school districts border. Every other year Gilman has a home game against Tri-County, and it is traditionally the Homecoming basketball game. One exception was the year after I graduated, when the game between the two was on a Tuesday in December, and Homecoming is always on a Friday night after Christmas vacation. Also, when Gilman City played at Tri-County, it was usually their Homecoming game.

Gilman City and Tri-County have had some epic boys and girls basketball games. Even when one team is having a better season than the other, the underdog summons enough emotion and desire to make the game close. The rivalry has seen some big upsets, which I know from experience. The year before I played, when my brother Seth was a senior, Tri-County beat Gilman on Gilman's Homecoming on a last-second shot. Gilman City would finish 8-1 in HDC play that year and share the conference title. Tri-County would be a 5-4 also ran. Likewise, my sister has been playing tough games with the Mustangs since her days of 5th and 6th grade basketball, and continued to do so the years after I graduated.

Tri-County plays in a "modern era" HDC gym. Recently built, it features plastic seats, which are more comfortable than the wooden bleachers of old. Also, like many recently built gyms in the area, big I-beams run along the ceiling. It doesn't have the capacity some HDC gyms do, but it's a nice comfortable place to watch a game. The court is fairly nice as well, with good padding on the walls should a player go flying past the baseline.

Andy Lewis coached at Tri-County for several years before being replaced by Chris Hodge before my first year of high school basketball.

The Gilman City gym is a big part of the community's heritage. Community members have been playing and watching games there since the 1950s. It's a great place to play a game and a nice home court advantage.

Jamesport is known for the many Amish people who live around the town. The Amish presence combines with several shops downtown to give the town a considerable tourist industry. The Amish references carry over to basketball, as some Gilman City players refer to Tri-County teams as "the Amish." Once, Coach Burke saw the Tri-County players doing an interesting shooting drill before a game. He implemented it into our practices. Since we learned it from Tri-County, we call it the "Amish shooting drill." Long live rivalry.

All jokes aside, however, some kids at Gilman City are friends with kids from Jamesport, and some people from the two towns party together. Although players take immense pride in beating the other team, it's mostly a friendly rivalry.

Another traditional rival of Gilman City is the North Harrison Shamrocks of Eagleville. On years Gilman City doesn't have a home game with Tri-County, they host North Harrison, and that game is usually our Homecoming. We decorate the walls for Homecoming, and we have a heyday with the fact their mascot is a glorified weed. Although Gilman City is an agricultural community, the references to Roundup are a bit excessive.

North Harrison has similarities to Gilman as far as athletics are concerned. As far as basketball tradition from the game's roots in the area until the present, Gilman City and North Harrison are the tops in the conference. Like Gilman City, North Harrison has made several trips to the state Final Four. Several good players have come out of Eagleville, including a player on the 1966 NCAA Champion Texas Western team. North Harrison teams usually have big rosters, as lots of the students there play basketball.

Also, North Harrison plays in an older gym with wooden bleachers, like Gilman City. These two gyms are cathedrals, grand old shrines to the game and to their respective towns. In the tradition and atmosphere departments, these two gyms are the best in the HDC, in my opinion.

North Harrison's gym probably has the highest capacity in the HDC. With a huge stack of wooden bleachers on one side and more rising on the other side, it outsizes the other gyms in the conference, except maybe the domed curiosity at Pattonsburg. On the wall of the North Harrison gym giant, imposing green letters spell out "NHHS."

Eagleville is a small town that sits on Interstate 35, near the Iowa border. Eagleville stands out for two reasons: the town's fireworks stores and the Dinner Bell Café. In large part because Iowa controls fireworks like they are cocaine, Eagleville is full of huge, year-round fireworks stores. My friends and I often make pilgrimages to the Dinner Bell to eat at the truck stop restaurant. $1.99 gets you a massive homemade cinnamon roll, my personal favorite.

East of Eagleville, also near the Iowa border, sits the North Mercer School. It sits in the small town of Mercer, amidst the hilly terrain that makes up Mercer County. With the conference tournament, districts, and the regular season game, Gilman City played Mercer three times a year each year I played high school basketball. This familiarity, combined with the fact Mercer fielded some very good teams during my playing days, made Mercer often take the role of Bugs Bunny to my Elmer Fudd. Wins over Mercer were an achievement not to be taken lightly.

Over the last 10 years, the North Mercer basketball teams have ranged from good to dominant. In the six years from my 7th grade year to graduation, the North Mercer girls' basketball team lost a grand total of two regular season HDC games. The North Mercer boys' team has finished in the top three in the conference for as long as I can remember.

One reason for the success of North Mercer is the town has a few families in which all members play basketball, usually with success. Brothers, sisters, cousins, and parents all play basketball, providing the school with players for long periods of time. All teams in Mercer's recent run of success have had at least one Stark, Martin, Wilson, Hague, or Brundage.

North Mercer has also had good coaches. Stacy Snyder coached the girls during my playing career, while Dan Owens and then Nathan Hinrichs coached the boys' team. In addition to these coaches' ability to prepare their teams, they share an affinity for antics on the sidelines, especially Owens and Snyder. These coaches would unleash a verbal barrage on players and referees when things went awry. Technical fouls were just a by-product. They also would exhort the crowd for support at key junctures in the game. Once, a North Mercer player made a big three, prompting Owens to do a backstroke in mid-air to rally the crowd. These coaches brought intensity to the game. Off the court, however, they're all really nice people.

North Mercer plays in a new gym with plastic seats, similar to the one at Tri-County, except Mercer has seats on both sides of the court. Above the section where Mercer fans sit, red letters on the wall spell "The 6th Man," in reference to the supportive fans.

North Mercer players, though very competitive, mostly seemed like nice people. Mercer girls always took care to make sure they had a good appearance off the court. Gilman boys took care to notice.

Southeast of Mercer, in probably the most remote outpost of the HDC, is the Newtown-Harris School. The school is in the town of Newtown, with the town of Harris being a few miles to the south. In Sullivan County, Newtown is in very hilly country, far removed from bigger towns with Wal-Marts and movie theaters.

My family raised cattle in this area before I was born and until I was one and a half years old. In the late '80s, we moved to Nebraska. After about eight years there, we moved to the farm where we live now, on a gravel road between Gilman City and Coffey. My parents made good friends with several families in the area. My dad always says the people there are as good as any to be found. Whenever we play Newtown, my parents visit a lot with their old friends.

Newtown just joined the HDC my junior year. We also played them in a non-conference game my sophomore year. They filled in as a Homecoming opponent after a flu outbreak at North Harrison forced our game with them to be postponed.

For a long time, Tim Cool has coached the Newtown basketball teams. Because of his name and his composure in big, close games, people have said Newtown "stays Cool" under pressure. Jeremy Parsons coached the girls' team and was an assistant on the boys' team. Likewise, Cool was an assistant for the girls' team. When I played against Cool's teams I was always struck by how much they played as a team. Newtown teams usually are solid fundamentally and hustle well.

The Newtown-Harris Tigers play in a gym with wooden bleachers and a court that has a surface that looks like Legos. The surface is made of hard plastic or rubber. It doesn't affect the game any unless you fall, in which case you get odd-looking red marks on your knees and arms. There's only about a foot of out of bounds space all around the court, creating an intense, Arena Football affect.

South of Newtown-Harris is the Grundy R-V School at Galt. The Grundy Panthers had a mini rivalry with Gilman City when my brother played. His senior year, the two schools shared the HDC regular season title. Gilman's only HDC loss that year was that odd Homecoming setback against Tri-County. Grundy's loss came in the head-to-head contest between the two schools. Jacob Wilson gave Gilman the win with a last-second jumper. The year before, he beat Grundy on another last-second jumper, from nearly the same spot, to win 3rd in the HDC Tournament. Unfortunately, Grundy beat Gilman in the District Championship in my brother's senior year, which was also my freshman year. Gilman City and Grundy had very good teams at the same time, enhancing the rivalry.

Adding to the rivalry was Grundy fans' long history of annoying people from Gilman, and vice versa. Once, Gilman City second graders dressed up as cheerleaders for a game and did cheers. Grundy fans booed them. Adults. Booed. Second graders. When my classmate Kaleb Wilson was keeping stats for the high school team, he stuck his tongue out at Grundy coach Les Jackson. Also, there was a game or two Gilman played at Grundy when people said the officiating seemed heavily in Grundy's favor. I don't blame officials for a loss and Gilman actually ended up winning the game, but there have been a few complaints through the years that Grundy hired "hometown referees."

All things considered, however, Grundy has had success under coach Jackson. Jackson, like Cool at Newtown, was an establishment at Grundy during my career, having coached the school a long time. The year Grundy narrowly defeated Gilman City in the district championship, the Panthers went all the way to the state quarterfinals.

Grundy plays in a modern-era gym, similar to the gyms at Tri-County and Mercer. It was the site of the HDC Tournament my senior year.

Like with Grundy, Gilman City and Ridgeway's teams have seemed to be in the same situation at the same time during the time I played basketball. In junior high, we both had good teams and played good games. Both schools had down years when kids my age first started playing high school basketball. Then, my junior and senior years, we both had good teams, so we often played close games. The Owls had some good scorers, so they always provided good competition.

My senior year and in the years after, Ridgeway did not have a girls high school basketball team. This upsets me because it takes games away from the Gilman City girls' schedule. It's also a troubling sign for a high school when it can't find five girls willing to make the commitment to play basketball.

But the boys' team always provided good competition for us. Ridgeway fans could be rowdy and annoying, but that made for good game atmospheres. It was fun to do something good to silence them. However, the excessive whining to the referees by some Ridgeway players did get old.

The Ridgeway Owls play in a barn-like structure. The court is tile and the walls are close to the court. The seats are wooden and painted gray, and big wooden roof support poles obstruct the view of fans. The visitors' locker rooms are up a rickety flight of ancient wooden stairs; tiny, cramped lofts overlooking the court.

For a long while, Tom Hogan coached Ridgeway. My senior year, Lee Rucker became the basketball coach. He appeared to be a good coach and his teams played the style that was right for his players, which was up-tempo and centered around three-pointers.

Near Ridgeway, in central Harrison County, is the Cainsville School. The Cainsville Redmen and Redettes haven't had tremendous success in the past few years. However, the school has produced some good players through the years. Cainsville didn't have a boys' basketball team my senior year, but they have every other year.

I only played at Cainsville once. Unfortunately, Cainsville's gym joins Ridgeway's and North Daviess' in the lower tier of gyms in the HDC. It has a tile floor, and the bleachers are old, chipped wood. The bleachers don't have much in the stair department, and navigating them is tricky. Also, the wood on the bleachers isn't connected, it's just planks on a frame. Therefore, unattended items can fall through the cracks and land below the bleachers, like sand through a sifter. However, a basketball court is a basketball court, and I shouldn't complain. Also, the people of Cainsville make it a nice, quaint little town. The school blends into the HDC landscape.

Tri-County is one of four HDC schools in Daviess County. The others are North Daviess, Pattonsburg, and Winston.

North Daviess High School is located southwest of Gilman City in the town of Jameson. The Jameson Huskies and the Coffey Wolves consolidated to form the North Daviess Knights.

North Daviess gym is a substandard parody of a real gym. The floor is made of the same Lego material as the court at Newtown-Harris. North Daviess' court is much shorter than a regular court and there are about six inches of out of bounds territory all the way around the court. This basically makes the walls the out of bounds, creating the Arena Football feel. To inbound the ball, a player has to stand against a wall while everyone else stays behind a restraining line a few feet into the court. Players sit on the edge of the stage at the side of the court and fans are jammed into old bleachers on the stage behind them. However, I can't criticize the old gym too much because it was the site of one of my best statistical games. I had 26 points and 19 rebounds in our blowout win there.

Gilman's boys' team may never play there again because North Daviess hasn't had a boys' basketball team since my junior year.

While the girls' team has had a few years around .500, the boys' team hasn't been very good for a while. When the Knights earned their first win in a few years one year by defeating Winston, it touched off a wild celebration.

Near the North Daviess school is Pattonsburg. Pattonsburg sits right on I-35, like Eagleville. The town used to be a few miles down the road in the Grand River bottom, but it always got flooded. The great Flood of '93 was the last straw, and the entire town was moved a few miles up the road to higher ground, similar to the way Bancroft moved a mile north to be on the railroad and became Gilman City a century earlier.

Because of this history of flooding and the town's proximity to the Grand River, people from other schools sometimes call Pattonsburg the "River Rats." It's a term of endearment.

This move resulted in new school and athletic facilities for the Pattonsburg Panthers. They built a futuristic-looking dome for their gym, surrounded by smaller domes that have school classrooms. The inside of the massive basketball dome has an impressive view of the dome ceiling, which is rimmed with lights. Several rows of green plastic seats are on each side of the court, giving the gym a bigger capacity. The bouncing of the ball and the crowd noise are echoed in the dome, making the gym always seem louder than it really should be. The Pattonsburg dome was the site of the district tournaments my junior and senior year. I also played two regular season games there, so I have a lot of experience playing in the dome. The Pattonsburg teams that play in the dome are usually somewhere near the middle of the HDC pack.

The school farthest to the south in the HDC is Winston. During my career, Eric Lewis, the brother of the former Tri-County coach, coached Winston. Eric and Andy's dad, Nylon Lewis, was my dad's coach when he played. Eric has been the coach at Winston for a long time and is an influential person in the conference. Lewis' teams were always solid fundamentally and were known for the way they hustled. They played good defense, often playing tight zone defenses against us that forced us to earn our points. They also played with good sportsmanship and respect for the game of basketball, which I admired.

Winston plays in an older gym with wooden seats, similar to the gyms at Gilman City and North Harrison. The court has a few dead spots where the ball doesn't bounce great, but I didn't dribble much as a post player so it wasn't a big deal for me.

Winston was usually near the top of the HDC when I played, especially in my later years. They were always a challenge to play, but it was fun to play them.

These 11 schools—Gilman City, Tri-County, North Harrison, North Mercer, Newtown-Harris, Grundy R-V, Ridgeway, Cainsville, North Daviess, Pattonsburg, and Winston—make up the HDC conference. It's sports small-town style, with rivalries, supportive fans, and tradition. Playing sports in the HDC is also about pride. Each town develops a reputation and a character that makes it different from all the other small towns. Family names synonymous with their towns provide their schools with talent for generations. The player, coaches, fans, and gymnasiums all play a part in the making of the unique tapestry of HDC athletics.

CHAPTER 3

The first weeks of high school basketball practices were brutal, used for conditioning to get into shape for the upcoming season. The endless running and drills of early-season practices were my introduction to high school basketball. What I noticed early on was the heightened intensity of high school basketball compared to junior high sports and even high school softball. I loved how important it was, how success in high school basketball was a big accomplishment, something worth working and practicing for. When you seem like a somewhat insignificant person in a somewhat insignificant town, you are enthralled by the opportunity to achieve something lasting and important.

At the same time, practices had plenty of lighter moments, like the steady stream of jokes, the not-very-good Coach Burke impersonations, or the time Sawyer DeWitt twisted his socks after practice, producing a cascade of accumulated sweat. They were sometimes fun, such as when we scrimmaged or did fast-break drills. It was fun to just play basketball, a release after a day of classes.

I first experienced high school practices as a sophomore. At Gilman City, freshmen usually play junior high basketball. Players are eligible to play a full junior high season and half of the high school season, which they sometimes do to get a taste of the high school level. In years where there is a lack of depth or an exceptionally talented freshman, the frosh will play the full high school season instead of junior high.

There were four kids in my class of eight who played basketball, Kaleb Wilson, Heath Oram, Sawyer, and myself. We were pretty good players for freshmen, but we played junior high because the high school roster was full of upperclassmen. We did get experience playing with the seniors in pickup games because Kaleb and I had older brothers who were seniors when we were freshmen. My older brother, Seth, played on the high school team, as did Kaleb's older brother, Jacob Wilson.

We had a successful junior high team while the senior-laden high school team won 20 games, the Gilman City Tournament, the HDC regular season title, took third in the HDC Tournament, and finished 2nd in the District Tournament.

Gilman City had other successful sports teams during my freshman year. I was on the softball team that took 2nd in the state. After a so-so regular season, the team rallied to reel off several wins in the state tournament in Chillicothe. We finished 2nd after losing the championship game to—arrgh—Grundy R-V. Other than the State Tournament run, my highlight of the season was when I went 4-for-4 against North Daviess on September 11, 2001.

I was also on the high school track team, although track isn't my strongest area. I was primarily a thrower, throwing the shot put all of 28'5" and the discus an underwhelming 83'1". These were my season highs, which I guess aren't too bad for a skinny freshman. Needless to say, however, I wasn't a track star. I did run a few distance races and once filled in as the anchor leg of the 4 X 400 meter relay. The real anchor leg runner wasn't at the South Harrison track meet, so coach Stan Tibbles asked me to fill in. To be honest, I'm not fast. But we were in a heat with only Pattonsburg and us. When I took the baton, (which we had borrowed from the Princeton girls' relay team when our baton mysteriously disappeared) I was only a few strides ahead of Pattonsburg's last runner. I fully expected to get blown away, but I somehow held on, even extending my lead. When I crossed the line I got to knock down the string held across the line, the illicit dream of slow runners everywhere. Even though our time didn't qualify us for the finals, winning the heat was a good memory.

The spring of my freshman year, I was on the golf team, the last year Gilman City had a golf team. We played this sport purely for the fun of it. At one golf meet, Kaleb and I played in a scramble-style competition, in which we could pick the better ball location and both hit from there. This allowed us to avoid embarrassingly high scores and to fearlessly hack shots out of ponds or tall grass while the other player used their shot to take a drop.

All these other sports were fun and competitive, but basketball is king at Gilman. It's the sport that has the longest season and that people care about the most. The four of us in my class, once we reached our sophomore year, would have our work cut out for us trying to follow up on the previous year's success, which had been the workings of that big class of 2002.

With only one starter, Jacob Webb, back for the 2002-03 season, we would be a young team. We had two seniors, both of whom had never played high school basketball before, three juniors, and four sophomores. The fate of the Gilman City hoops team was on our inexperienced shoulders.

Compounding our inexperience problem was Gilman City's demanding early season schedule. Gilman starts each season with many games against 2A and 3A schools, many of which are in the GRC and county seat towns. The schedule is demanding, and includes the highly competitive Gallatin Invitational Tournament. All things considered, however, I like playing a challenging non-conference schedule. It makes Gilman teams improve quicker than if we played lesser competition, and it does a great job of preparing us for HDC play. The only thing I would change about Gilman's schedule would be to add more games, because I like playing games.

The early-season practices aren't so enjoyable. Early practices are for conditioning, so it's basically running and footwork drills without much work with the ball. Early in each practice we would run stairs, going up to the highest row of seats, running over to the other side, down the stairs, back over, and then up again. We'd run lap after lap, waiting for Coach Burke to finally say, "Finish it out!" Upon this we would sprint to the water fountains. Practices always ended with us shooting 25 free throws for practice. Then we had each player shoot two free throws and all of us ran based on how many free throws were missed.

As we got farther along and closer to starting the season, practices got more interesting. We'd do fast break drills, more shooting drills, and began to work on our offenses and defenses. In addition to zone defenses and offenses, we worked a lot on the motion offense, which focused on timing and patience. We even worked some with a triangle offense and a 1-4 offense. When Coach Burke started showing us some of those triangle sets, we realized this wasn't junior high ball anymore. My sophomore year I was 6'3" and by the time I graduated I was 6'4" or 6'5", so I was always the 4 or 5 in our offensive sets. I enjoyed playing the post. It's such a battle of wills and decision-making, as in the all-out effort for a rebound or deciding how to attack based on the defense. Most of us picked up on the plays quickly.

We also worked on several inbounds plays, ranging from the ultra traditional stack and box plays to the exotic "Kentucky" in bounds play. When running "Kentucky," we started in a bunch on the perimeter and scattered out towards the ball like Texas Tech wide receivers.

When we scrimmaged, I was usually matched up against Tony Tenhulzen. He was big and strong enough to play good post defense. He was a senior, but was in his first year playing basketball. He improved a lot as the season went on.

Eventually, after weeks of practice, our first game was at hand. Before our first game, we had the traditional meet the coaches and players night. People come to eat and then the players are introduced. Coaches talk a little about the upcoming season and then we have a brief scrimmage. Unfortunately, Sawyer hurt his ankle kind of bad a few seconds into the scrimmage. After we helped him off the court I noticed his ankle looked sort of misshapen. He would end up missing a few games to start the season but would recover nicely from the injury.

Our first game was supposed to be at home against Princeton. However, Princeton was in the state football playoffs, so our game with them was postponed for a few weeks. We would start the season with the Gallatin Invitational Tournament. We were seeded No. 7 in the eight-team tourney, so we would play the No. 2 seed South Harrison Bulldogs. South Harrison High School was located in Bethany, the Harrison County seat, and was a 2A school. Gilman City was, of course, a 1A school.

A few days before the game I learned I would be a starter. It would be the first of the 80 games I would start and play in for Gilman City. I had figured I had a good chance to start because I had played well in practice and was the tallest player on the team. I was pretty much the tallest player in the HDC when I played. I was also the youngest player on our team; until my birthday on January 23 I was the only 15-year-old on the team.

It was tough to be prepared for our game with South Harrison when only one player on our team, Jacob Webb, had played meaningful minutes at the high school level. However, we were excited to start the season and to start getting experience. Beyond that, we weren't sure what to expect. There was a feeling of anticipation on the bus ride down to Gallatin. Ready or not, when we walked onto the floor in Gallatin's big gym, our season had begun.

South Harrison exploited its size advantage early in the game. I was tall but skinny and South Harrison had big players who had bulked up for football. The player guarding me, Ryan Madison, would go on to play football at the University of Missouri as a lineman. I battled in the post, however, fighting for position and grabbing some rebounds.

We struggled offensively during the game. The talented and physical Bulldogs disrupted what we had run in scrimmages. We lost badly, 70-26. It was never really very close.

I finished with five points and five rebounds. Three of my points came on free throws. My only field goal was a memorable one, however. I got the ball in the high post just inside the free throw line. I dribbled once, spun to my left, and let fly a 14-foot hook shot that splashed through the net. It was a little lucky, but it looked good. It was an important moment in my career because it helped me realize I needed to make the hook shot a big part of my game. People came up to me after the game and complimented me on my hook shot, while remaining too polite to mention we had lost by 44 points. Although it didn't really change the outcome of that game, the hook shot did make me realize what a weapon it could be if I worked on it. You can get a shot off over anyone with a good hook shot.

We had to shake off the loss quickly because we moved into the loser's bracket and now had to play Tri-County, our rival and one of the teams in the upper third of the conference that year. The game with the Mustangs was much closer, as we stayed within 10 points for much of the game with a scrappy effort. I contributed some rebounds and made a few lay-ups, finishing with six points. The other starters were playing steady games as well. We were also getting good contributions from our bench, but we couldn't quite seem to draw even.

In the second half, Tri-County was trying to put us away when one of our guards, junior Matt Houser, did it for them. Matt was

The 2002-03 Gilman City Hawks, my first year of high school basketball.
Front row from left: Heath Oram, Darrin Elder, Daniel Prindle, Sawyer DeWitt,
and Jacob Webb. Back row from left: Matt Houser, Tony Tenhulzen, Coach Brent
Burke, Benjamin Herrold and Kaleb Wilson.

called for a foul as a Tri-County player shot. Never a portrait of restraint, Matt yelled, "What!?!" and started yelling at the refs. They gave him a technical. Now a technical foul is the universal sign for a player or coach to shut up, but Matt went for broke. He kept yelling and griping about the call, earning a second T and an ejection. As he was walking to our locker room he tried to pick up the ball and throw it. He slipped on a wet spot on the court and fell. The hushed crowd stifled laughter. When Matt finally made it off the court, the gym was silent as we all tried to fathom the ridiculousness of what had just happened.

Tri-County's Byron King then made six free throws in a row, two for the foul and two apiece for the technicals. I still wonder if it's legal or if it's a record that one team shot six straight free throws.

Tri-County also got the ball, and they were on a roll the rest of the game, draining threes and turning the game into a rout as we continued to struggle to score. When the game mercifully came to an end, we had lost 70-33. Matt was suspended for two games, one for each technical.

Sitting at 0-2 and having lost by 44 and 37 points, it seemed like it could be a long season. But it was still early in the season and we were gaining experience with each game, so nobody on the team was too upset. We had played two good teams and were still focused on improving as a team and as individual players.

A new addition to the GIT was the 7th place game, meaning the two teams that lost their first two games of the tournament would play each other, giving every team in the tournament three games. It was a good idea, especially for an early-season tournament.

We played Winston in the 7th place game, another young team struggling early in the season. It was a breakout game for the team and for myself. Our offense finally got going and we finally held an opponent to under 70 points. We got to experience the other end of a blowout, winning 64-37. It was a good boost to the team's confidence, proof that our work in practice could pay off. I scored 18 points on 7-of-9 shooting while pulling down nine rebounds. I used my height advantage to control the post. I hadn't been a real prolific scorer in junior high, as my scoring topped out at 8.4 points per game my freshman year. To be honest, I was somewhat surprised I had been able to be as effective offensively as I was against Winston. I realized that game I could make meaningful offensive contributions for the team, perhaps do more than block shots and rebound.

Following the Gallatin Tournament was our first home game, a matchup with the Princeton Tigers of the GRC. Fresh off playing in the state football playoffs, Princeton had several big, physical players.

We showed we could be a scrappy team, hanging with the bigger, stronger Princeton team. I started the game having a good shooting night, finding just enough space to get off shots over and around Bret Cavanaugh, the All-Conference football player who was guarding me. Also, with Kaleb, Sawyer, Jacob, and Matt, we had fast players and we used our speed to negate their size. I wasn't real quick, but I ran the court and moved well for a post player, adding to our speed advantage.

In the second quarter, there was a scramble for a loose ball after one of our guards knocked the ball away from a Princeton player. I picked up the ball, eyeing an uncontested lay-up. However, a Princeton player bumped me and, as I sidestepped, my left ankle rolled and collapsed under me. The spraining of my ankle felt weird, like I'd tried to step on the floor and missed, only to have my leg buckle under me. A foul was called and we were in the bonus, so I had two free throws.

It hurt to put a lot of weight on the ankle, but I wanted to shoot the free throws I had earned, so I walked it off. Eventually I could put weight on it. Standing mostly on one leg, I made both free throws and kept playing. It got better as I played on it. It didn't hurt really badly until I stopped moving on it after the game was over. We were hanging in the game, too, which made me focus on just playing basketball.

At halftime, I realized I probably should have wrapped the ankle or something, because the ankle wanted to twitch and was sore. However, when we started playing in the second half I put weight on it and it felt okay. The real problem in the second half was our offense went cold. After a good shooting first half, nobody could hit down the stretch. Princeton pulled away in the latter stages of the game and we lost 53-35. I finished with 15 points, but I was upset we let the game slip away late. Also, my ankle started swelling after the game.

I went home and put a bag of frozen peas on my ankle, which helped contain the swelling. However, when I went to bed I couldn't put covers over my ankle because it hurt too much. Needless to say, I didn't sleep really well that night.

In the morning it was stiff and sore and I had to go down the steps one at a time while sitting down. Each time I moved the throbbing ankle ached. I think what caused the sprain and made it as bad as it was was that most of us had ordered adidas a3 shoes. Although they were good shoes overall, they were really thick on the sides and kind of low. When you hit the ground off balance, if your ankles weren't strong enough, the shoes would roll on their side. The only time I ever rolled my ankle was wearing these shoes.

Most of the time when things are sore in the morning they feel better a few hours into the day, so I went into school the next day a few hours late. It felt better by mid-morning, so I went on into school. It even stood the test of going up to the school's third floor where most of my classes were located. By afternoon, the ankle loosened up and didn't hurt very bad. Although it would be sore for a few weeks afterwards, it wouldn't be a big deal. Coach Burke would tape it before games, just for extra support.

We had a slightly longer layoff after the Princeton game, which gave us extra time to prepare for tough upcoming games with Hamilton and Gallatin. These were 3A and 2A schools, respectively. We played at Hamilton, a quality team with two big post players. It was an early test for me as to how I would do playing against some of the best post players in the area. We played a 2-3 zone to limit their post scoring and offensive rebounds. I used the hook shot to get shots off in the post, scoring 13 points and securing eight rebounds. Despite our efforts, Hamilton was too talented and experienced for us. We lost 69-36. We did play hard until the end, which should count for something.

The game at home against Gallatin was a rerun of the Hamilton game. We lost 81-51 to fall to 1-5 on the season. I again scored 13 points, a good sign in that I was developing as a player but a bad sign in that I was powerless to keep my team from being routed.

We had a chance to get some momentum going into Christmas break in our final game before the break. We played our first HDC contest at Pattonsburg, a winnable game. Christmas break was a 2-3 week span with no games, only practices. A win heading into the break would make it seem like we had turned the corner. A loss would send us into the break on a four-game losing streak.

Pattonsburg would finish near the bottom of the HDC that year, but they had a good outside shooter in Tyler Miller. We started slowly offensively (again) while Miller poured in points for Pattonsburg. His teammates seemed to feed off his shooting, leading to a barrage of three-pointers, which stretched the Panthers' lead to nearly 20. We went to a box and one defense in the second half, in which four of us played zone defense while one defender always shadowed Miller. It slowed down Pattonsburg, but the damage was done. We were unable to reel them in, leading to a 51-35 loss. After respectable performances against the tough competition of Hamilton and Gallatin, I played poorly against Pattonsburg. I scored only seven points in the frustrating loss. The loss showed how far we still had to progress as a team to be successful.

We limped into Christmas break at 1-6 and 0-1 in HDC play. Four of our six losses were by 30 or more points. We had experienced offensive struggles, scoring 36 points or less in five of our seven games. We had plenty to work on in our practices over the break.

However, the early-season games had yielded some positive things. We had earned high school basketball experience, and had played against tough competition, which had us more prepared for conference play. We had shown spurts of being a high-scoring team. We were also developing as individual players. Kaleb and Sawyer were learning to use their athleticism and to rebound. Our primary guards, Jacob, Heath, and Matt, were improving their outside shooting and ability to handle the presses other teams tried against us. Daniel Prindle was becoming a solid contributor off the bench. I was learning how to work in the post, when to use certain moves and how to find open teammates when defenses collapsed. Most post scoring was improving quickly. People around the school and town had noticed my play and were talking with me about basketball. Basketball was something I was becoming known for, something to go with my reputation for getting good grades. While high school at Gilman City isn't the social cauldron it is at some bigger schools, it helps to have something you're known for. Success at basketball is a surefire way to earn respect at the school and in the community due to Gilman's basketball tradition and the attention the sport receives in the area.

However, individual success means little in basketball when your team is 1-6. The bottom line was that we had been a very bad team so far, and we needed to improve drastically. We worked hard over the break in an attempt to add to our lonely win column. That remained our focus heading into January: win games. Or at least "win a game" would work in this situation.

CHAPTER 4

Christmas Break is just that, a break from school and from basketball games. (That was until Gilman City joined the NCMC Holiday Classic a few years after I played.) For players, the break is filled with practices, family dinners, and watching college football. The parade of practices seems to drag on, but they are important due to the lineup of conference games immediately after the break.

Still, it was tough for us not to play flat and to practice with intensity with so many practices in the middle of the season without a game. Focus is important, but that isn't always easy for teenage boys to do. Occasionally, Coach Burke would have to stop the practice to "encourage" us to pick up the intensity. Also, a heavy dose of Christmas dinners followed by a heavy dose of running in practice leads to an increase in mid-practice trips to the trashcan.

One break in the practice routine came when we all got to go down to Columbia to watch Missouri play Valparaiso. Coach Burke got free tickets for the team, and it was a fun trip to take as a team. I liked watching MU's Arthur Johnson, who was a post player who wore #50, like me. I learned some things about playing the post by watching him play. After watching the high-level college players, we were motivated to improve our team in the post-break part of the season.

One problem facing our team as we resumed play after the break was a shortage of leadership. Because our team relied almost entirely on young and inexperienced players during my sophomore season, we didn't have too many vocal leaders on the team. The only leader early in the season was Jacob Webb, a junior, who had started on the conference championship team the year before. He helped keep players focused in most of our practices. He also was a leader in games. His comments were basically limited to "C'mon!" and "Let's Go!" However, they were both reminders to pick up the intensity. They could be directed at an individual or the whole team, and they basically translated to this insightful advice: "Play better!"

Jacob and I were the highest scorers on the team that year. However, like most of the players on the team, I was still learning the ways of high school basketball and was too focused on learning the plays and working on my game to be much of a verbal leader. I was only a sophomore, so I didn't talk much in the huddle anyway. Not to mention I was too busy guzzling water during timeouts to say much anyway. While I was more quiet and reserved, Jacob was more extroverted and was a central figure in Gilman City high school society, which combined with his playing experience to make him good for a leadership role on our team.

At 1-6, we were a team in need of direction heading into our first game after the break, a home game with Cainsville. Gilman City always has very supportive home crowds. Despite our poor record, this year was no exception. People in the community had remained encouraging and positive despite our early-season struggles, at least when I was around them. They realized we were a young, rebuilding team and we played scrappy, hustling basketball. Even when we lost, people around town appreciated it when we played hard. That was enough for now. With our inexperience, we were a clean-slate team that had shown signs that it could be good in the future.

So, with the crowd behind us, we picked up a much-needed 51-40 win over Cainsville. The win put us at 1-1 in HDC play. It was a feel-good win, a sign we might have turned the corner and our work over the break had paid off. I had the first double-double of my career that night, with 18 points and 10 rebounds. I also had the best shooting night of my young career, making eight of my nine shots. The double-digit win was an encouraging way to start our post-break season.

Unfortunately, we followed the win with another losing streak. Our progression went backwards into regression with a 23-point home loss to Albany and an ugly 49-43 loss at Polo. We followed up the back-to-back losses with a 59-44 loss at Tri-County that dropped us to 1-2 in HDC play and 2-9 overall. The Tri-County loss was especially painful, as it was our second loss on the year to our biggest rival. Tri-County's guards were too quick and experienced for us to handle. We had some team speed as well, but the Mustangs did a better job harnessing and controlling their speed.

One of the few highlights of the loss was when I got a tremendous block, one of the best of my career. With my height, I blocked a lot of shots. But shot blocking also requires a lot of timing and quickness. For every block I got, there were times when I would flail helplessly at a ball out of my reach or the shooter would get me with a head fake. This time, however, I hit pay dirt with a block. Byron King, one of Tri-County's quick guards but also very short, had the temerity to drive the lane and try to lay one in right in front of me. I swung at the ball at it hit my wrist just as he released it. I spiked the ball into the court as hard as I could, completing the block with a flourish. It drew lots of cheers, but the Mustangs had the last laugh with their win. I scored 11 points in the game, but my team needed more from me it we were to pull the upset. Matt Houser had a nice game with several points and some steals. By the end of a night of the requisite partying, Matt was telling people he'd had 15 steals in the game.

The loss at Tri-County left us at 2-9 and on a three-game losing streak heading into our homecoming game with North Harrison. After a flu outbreak left North Harrison's teams unable to play, we re-scheduled our games with them and arranged a game with Newtown to be the Homecoming game.

Many of my most memorable high school memories are related to Homecoming Week. The Homecoming game is on a Friday, but the week starts with each class decorating a section of the walls leading to the gym. Each day of the week is a different dress up day for students, such as dressing like people in a certain decade, or dressing like cowboys, fairy tale characters, or senior citizens. Friday is always blue-and-white day, with prizes given for the best attire each day.

Once, high school activity picture day was on a Homecoming dress up day, so the National Honor Society had a pirate, an Indian, a cowboy, and Tinkerbelle in it. Gilman City had to be the first high school in America to have an activity picture day on a Homecoming dress up day. Other Homecoming activities through the years included smashing an old car and a cake-decorating contest.

Homecoming week culminates with an hour-long pep rally. The cheerleaders do cheers, the coaches talk about the game, and representatives from each class participate in games. In addition, the elementary classes make little floats and have a parade around the gym. There is also the class competition for the Spirit Stick. Each class responds to a cue from the cheerleaders by yelling "V-I-C-T-O-R-Y! That's our Gilman battle cry!" The loudest class wins the Spirit Stick. The elementary grades are usually grouped together, resulting in a high-pitched din of tiny voices. A few teachers do the highly subjective judging, with the senior class usually winning.

Each class puts on a short skit, ranging from the absurd (my class our sophomore year: a Gilman City Hawk beats up superheroes) to the nerdy (junior year: a Gilman City-Tri-County academic meet erupts into violence, with Blade Landes being a tae-kwon-do hawk who beats up Mustangs) to the hilarious (senior year: American Idol competition, a hawk wins it by dancing). That senior year Gilman City Idol skit, invented just a few hours before the pep rally, will go down as one of the best Homecoming skits of all time despite having little or no tie to that year's Homecoming theme. We each sang a few lines of a song and then faced ludicrously harsh criticism from the judges, class sponsors Coach Burke and Mr. Kaden, as well as classmate Hannah Kunkel. Kaleb sang and danced to some of a Britney Spears song, Krystal Huff bawled her way through "Crazy," Sawyer and Blade rocked out, and I sang the "Star Spangled Banner." After an intentionally hideous performance, I held the final "brave" for nearly 10 seconds, bringing down the house. Blade wrote in the senior class program that my performance was his most memorable moment through high school. Heath ended the skit by coming out as the dancing hawk, culminating his moves by pulling off his shirt. Skits such as this one show the lengths otherwise normal people go to in the name of school spirit.

Skits like these add to the festivity of Homecoming week. An equally essential, yet much more reverential, part of the week is the Homecoming king and queen ceremony. Each high school class and the basketball teams have king and queen nominees. With our small class of eight students, we just about took turns being candidates during the four years of high school. My classmates would have elected me as a nominee our sophomore year, but I declined, passing the opportunity on to the other candidate for the spot, Blade.

It was supposedly an honor to be a candidate and our queen candidate, Desiree Howe, was a nice enough girl, but it wasn't really something I cared to do. I didn't really want to rent a tux. Also, I didn't care to have such a large role in the coronation ceremony, which I respect as a school tradition but still think is a little overblown. I just wanted to play in the game and then hold a candle for the ceremony, as all the basketball players did. Basically, I wanted to stick to the roles I knew and enjoyed. I did this much of the time in high school. Dez was a little upset with me for causing her to be a candidate with Blade, who wasn't really popular and was often made fun of. However, when Homecoming night came, it seemed they both got more enjoyment out of being candidates than I would have.

For all the ceremony and celebration around Homecoming, the biggest part is the actual games, around which everything is centered. It was the last year before Newtown-Harris joined the HDC, so it was good to get a chance to play them before they became conference competition. Newtown had some quick scorers, such as Nick Collins and Kyle Fordyce.

A huge crowd was on hand for the game, one that required extra bleacher seats to be set up on the stage, across from the permanent seats. Besides the big Gilman Homecoming crowd, Newtown had a strong contingent of loyal fans cheering on their Tigers. The game was close throughout, with the fans' cheers rising and falling with the ebb and flow of the game. The atmosphere was great. When one of us would shoot a shot, the ball would hang in the air as the players jockeyed for position. The moment a shot would go in the crowd would erupt with noise, as if the shooter had set off a hundred fire alarms at once. It's an empowering feeling when you know what you do will affect so many people watching you. My memories of that night are almost surreal, the intense struggle, the big shots, the thunderous crowd interrupted by that odd silence during free throws. I was addicted to the importance of every game we played. Both teams always wanted to win so badly, even nonconference games such as this one.

I was having just a so-so game, and would finish with only eight points and nine rebounds. However, Daniel Prindle, a junior who came off the bench, had the game of his life. He was in the zone, keeping us in the game. Daniel would average 1.7 ppg on the year, but he had about 15 or 16 points that night, while playing in his signature bright yellow shoes.

With just a few seconds left in the game, we had the ball but trailed by three. Coach Burke called a timeout to draw up our last gasp play. Now, we weren't a very good 3-point shooting team. We would only shoot 21% from beyond the arc for the year. In the huddle Burke drew up a play to get Jacob a three from the corner. Jacob would make 25% of his 111 3-point attempts on the year.

The play worked as Jacob came off a double screen and launched a three from the corner. The buzzer went off as the shot swished through the net. Pandemonium. Overtime.

Our wild celebration was short-lived, unfortunately, as Newtown dominated the overtime period. We couldn't hit shots when we needed them and took a tough 54-48 loss. Following the dramatic game, the coronation and dance seemed anticlimactic, as when Tri-County stunned Gilman with a buzzer beater in the Homecoming game the year before.

To play well and tie the game at the buzzer only to lose in overtime is frustrating. We were now a woeful 2-10 on the year heading into our tournament, the Gilman City Invitational Tournament. We were also mired in an unsightly four-game losing streak.

The Gilman Invitational Tournament is one of the events that mark the passage of time on the town's social calendar. There's the Homecoming game, the graduation ceremonies and alumni banquet in May, the Gilman City Fair in July, the Christmas tree lighting ceremony in December at the park on the corner of Broadway and Main, and the Gilman Tournament, which takes up a week in late January. From the hardcore hoops fans that go to watch the games nearly every night to those who only come when Gilman plays, fans flock to the gym during the week. Between the local radio and newspaper coverage out of Bethany and Trenton and other schools' fans coming to Gilman City, the town enjoys much more attention than it is accustomed to. My dad's team won the Gilman Tournament when he played, and my brother's team had won it when he was a senior, in 2002. I wanted to join the club.

We played the Ridgeway Owls in the first round of the tournament. Ridgeway, like our team, had several young players trying to find success at the high school level. In Levi Price and Aaron Fitzpatrick they had some very good 3-point shooters, which the team focused its offense around.

Our team felt sluggish before the game. The other games were finishing early that night, so our game started earlier than it was supposed to, which caught us off guard. We started the game slowly, unable to find ways to score very much. I didn't score at all in the first half. At halftime, though, something changed. I think we all were sick of losing and decided to step up. We knew we could and should beat Ridgeway. We all played better in the second half. I went from being a nonfactor in the first half to being a dominator in the post, scoring 12 points in the second half. I also had 10 rebounds in the game. At the same time, our outside shots started falling. Sawyer used his leaping ability to get off good shots, contributing to our offensive surge. Perhaps most importantly, we were able to break their press without committing turnovers, which was often a problem against Ridgeway. Our revitalized play surged us into the lead and we held on to win 62-59.

The win set up our third meeting of the year with the Tri-County Mustangs, our biggest rival, in the tournament semifinal. I wasn't happy about being 0-2 against our rival so early in my career. Before the game, I happened to be watching the highlight video for the Lakers' 2000 championship. I was inspired by the way Shaq dominated and lifted his team with his size and determination. I wanted to play that way. I needed to play that way.

Tri-County was the No. 1 seed in the tournament. They jumped out to an early lead but we hung on. I used my size and the post moves I'd been working on to score 12 points in the first half. We were down at the half, but we weren't going away. At the half there was intensity in our locker room, a fire in us. We were ready to take control in the second half and pull the upset of the Mustangs.

We came out in the second half and began to cut into their lead. Tri-County coach Chris Hodge had his players try to front me throughout the game, but I usually just sealed off the defender in front of me and had my teammates lob it in over the top. With the precision passes from our guards, I could make the layup before more defensive help could get there.

However, my ankle rolled while playing defense. I couldn't really walk it off this time, so I came out for a few minutes to have our principal/athletic director Mr. Tolen wrap it up with tape. While I was out, other players stepped up to continue our rally. Heath hit an incredible reverse layup in traffic to cut the lead to four.

I reentered the game after a few minutes. As I had been throughout the game, I was in the zone down the stretch. I made the last five shots I took in the game. It was about as unstoppable as I have ever felt on a basketball court. It's a euphoric, thrilling, intoxicating feeling when you're playing your rival and the crowd's going crazy with each play and you're coming back and no matter what the defense does you just can't miss. Once, a defender hit the ball as I went up for a shot. It loosened my grip on the ball, but I still flipped the ball up and it went in. With each bucket by one of us Gilman City players, the crescendo of noise rose. We cut the lead to one. The old gym was shaking.

With about a minute to play and Tri-County leading by one, the Mustangs had the ball. Ryan Rosenbaum missed a baseline shot and I grabbed the rebound. I handed the ball to a guard and ran down the court.

I got position in the post, sealing my defender in front of me. With less than 30 seconds to play, Jacob lobbed the ball in to me. I jumped up, grabbed the ball, and laid it in the hoop. We were up by one. I yelled as loud as I could in celebration but my voice was lost in the din of the crowd that could feel a victory in its grasp. We were on the cusp of one of the biggest upsets in the recent history of Gilman City basketball.

Tri-County wasn't going to give up, however. They got the ball into the post to Cory Wray, who had tried to guard me that night. He turned and shot. I reached my arm straight up and blocked the shot. One of my teammates grabbed the ball with a few seconds to go. Tri-County fouled so we had to inbound the ball. Kaleb inbounded the ball to Jacob and he was fouled. He had a one-and-one free throw situation. He missed the front end, but Mustangs' guard Wade Dixon lost the ball as he tried to get up the court for a last-second heave. The buzzer went off and the celebration began. Gilman City 51, Tri-County 50.

I ran across the court, yelling and pointing to our fans. I couldn't hear myself over the din of our crowd cheering the victory. We celebrated as a team for a moment, giving Coach Burke high-fives. Then we went through the "good game" line, congratulating the Mustang players on their tremendous effort that night. As we left the court, our crowd gave us one more ovation. We went to the locker room slowly, basking in the adoration of the crowd and the glory of the moment. We had beaten the tournament's top seed, our biggest rival.

Our locker room was jubilation. Jason Taggart and Ryan Hulett, who graduated the year before, came into the locker room to congratulate us. We were fired up, ready to play Princeton for the tournament championship.

After the game, in frustration, Cory Wray punched a wall, and pieces of the plaster wall fell. The janitors filled the hole the next day, but the spot they filled is smooth, while the rest of the wall is textured. The smooth part of the wall is a lasting reminder of that game and what we accomplished. It brings back memories of that night, the win, all the big shots we hit, and the thunderous cheers of the crowd that was making noise for us.

The game may have been our best as a team and my best individually of the season, if not of all three years I played. It was a breakthrough game for us. I finished with 22 points on 9-of-12 shooting. I had been unstoppable down the stretch when we needed it the most. The next day in P.E. class, Coach Burke said, "Monster game last night, Ben." The night after the game and the next day, all anyone could talk about was the game. Sawyer kept saying, "Yes, we beat Tri-County!" at regular intervals during the day.

Soon after our big win, however, our focus shifted to preparation for the championship game. Saturday night was our tournament championship game with Princeton. It was the first tournament championship experience for most of us on the team. Whether it was a letdown for us after the emotional win over Tri-County or just Princeton's talent, we started slowly. Princeton had a good team that year, with a balance of athletic guards and big post players.

We never got our offense going that night, losing 51-32. I didn't help the offensive problem any by only scoring five points. It was an anticlimactic letdown after our big win, but we still earned a second place finish in the tournament, much higher than our No. 5 seed. We had experienced a tournament championship game. Our Gilman Tournament experience was something to build on, a taste of high school basketball success and the fun that comes with it.

After our breakthrough performance in the tournament, we were 4-11 and entering the heart of the conference season. Next up was a home game against the HDC-leading Grundy R-V Panthers.

The Panthers were the heavy favorites and would go on to win the HDC that year. Their leader was the brilliant Andy Peterson, who could drill threes at a frightening rate and seemed to be able to fly. Grundy coach Les Jackson put him in the center of a 1-3-1 defense and let him block anything shot from within the gym.

However, we had confidence after our good showing in the Gilman Tournament. We weren't intimidated by any team, even if it was the best in the conference. We started out playing very well, staying with the Panthers and keeping Peterson under control. When I slipped behind the Grundy defense and put in a layup, we were ahead 9-8 and Coach Jackson called a timeout. The next few minutes were very different, unfortunately, and soon Coach Burke was the one who called for a timeout. The scoreboard read: Grundy R-V 22, Gilman City 9. Grundy's 14-0 run was fueled mostly by Peterson. Twice in the first half he had breakaways with only Matt Houser between him and the basket. Twice he jammed it home in Matt's face. Matt tried for payback with a one-on-one layup against Peterson, but Andy blocked the ill-fated attempt into the crowd.

That run was the difference in the game. After building a first-half lead, Grundy cruised to a 69-46 win, which dropped us to 4-12 and 1-3 in the HDC. A few of us had decent games, and I had a 10-point, 11-rebound double-double, but none of us could lift our team enough to keep up with the Peterson-led Panthers. Peterson would go on to play basketball at Northwest Missouri State University, an NCAA Division II school.

Our next game was at the other end of the HDC spectrum, the North Daviess Knights. It would be the only high school game against North Daviess for players in my class because the Knights wouldn't field a team for games with us my junior and senior years due to a lack of players. We did get to play our one North Daviess game at their court, the infamous "Lego." It was, if nothing else, a unique experience. With the court shorter than normal, the walls being the out of bounds territory, and fans jammed in bleachers on the stage next to the court, it's a claustrophobic setting. The action is confined to a smaller space due to size constraints, like at Martinsville Speedway or Fenway Park, only without the charm or quaintness.

Despite the unusual setting, we came out with the confidence a team has when facing the conference cellar dweller. Gilman City-North Daviess games have been ridiculously uncompetitive in recent years, with Gilman cruising to blowout wins. Jacob Wilson dunked it a few times in games with North Daviess, an awe-inspiring feat in the mostly below-the-rim HDC. Andy Terhune, for reasons unknown to anyone else, had tried to dunk against the Knights during his senior year, despite never dunking anything in his life. His inexplicable two-handed dunk attempt that was rejected by the front of the rim led to gym-wide laughter that lasted longer than a Cal Ripkin standing ovation. Andy's "dunk" is still talked about. ("Remember when Andy tried...")

This year's game was another blowout win for us, although North Daviess seemed to have a decent team that year. I was on a roll along

Working in the post against the Princeton Tigers in the 2003 Gilman City Tournament championship game.

with the team, grabbing rebounds, making shots, collected my misses (of which there were plenty) and putting them in. I would make just over 67% of my free throw attempts that year, but against North Daviess I made 10 of my 12 attempts, an 83.3 percentage. With our team rolling to a 76-32 victory, I finished with perhaps the best stat line of my life: 26 points and 19 rebounds. We were now 5-12 on the season, 2-3 in HDC play.

After the game, since it wasn't a school night, I went with Seth, Zack Ward, and Kaleb to the Dinner Bell restaurant in Eagleville. For some reason, it's incredibly fun to drive up to this little 24-hour truck stop café. Throughout high school, often after basketball games, my friends and I often went up there for late night snacks. The place has good mozzarella sticks and chicken strips, but I usually get the $1.99 Homemade cinnamon roll, a brick-sized pastry that's addictively good. Since we often went after basketball games, our conversations at the Dinner Bell were usually about the basketball team, with lengthy digressions about other sports, school, and a tremendous range of Seinfeld-like minutia.

Since Eagleville is home to several massive, year-round fireworks stores, we sometimes could talk Zack into buying fireworks for entertainment when we got back to Zack's house. We'd light bottle rockets and throw them in the air, light fireworks and throw them in a field of corn, creating a tremendous flash of light, or lay bottle rockets on a blacktop highway and have them race. Barring the time a Saturn Missile was set off on someone's porch in the middle of the night, it was all harmless fun. Other things we did for fun included campouts, which happened more when I was in junior high and almost always ended with us sleeping in a nearby living room.

Also, one of the biggest things we did was go to Royals games in Kansas City. They usually weren't very good but it was still a lot of fun to watch them play. Once, Zack, Seth, Kaleb, and I painted "KRIS" on our chests for a game since Kris Wilson was pitching for the Royals. Some guy outside the stadium said we should rearrange ourselves to spell out "RISK" because Kris Wilson had been a relief pitcher and was now starting. Before the game, Wilson warmed up in the outfield and then tossed his warmup ball to us in our outfield seats. Our letters got sunburned onto our skin and Wilson got shelled, but it was still a fun day at Kauffman Stadium.

Back on the basketball court, we had the HDC Tournament coming up. It was a big event on the schedule, a chance to build on our recent improvements and to show the rest of the conference what we could do.

CHAPTER 5

The HDC Conference Tournament, with its decades of tradition, is an event of historical and cultural significance for the small communities in northwest Missouri. The week of games is always one of the biggest parts of the regular season schedule. The games are an opportunity for players to show their skills to other players and fans from schools around the conference. When you play in these games, you have the attention of the whole conference.

The conference tournament is also a chance to socialize and meet with people from other schools. With most high schools in the area being small, students from different schools become part of a larger, loosely connected high school society that covers the HDC region. Students from different schools are friends or know each other through friends or acquaintances. The HDC Tournament is a confluence point for the HDC society, a place where this connected society comes together into full view. It's the place for HDC people to be, like the Oscars for Hollywood.

With our early season struggles, we had a play-in game with North Harrison, one of our rivals, to start our tournament games. A win would put us in the eight-team bracket. Six of the 11 HDC teams (four of 10 my sophomore year) play in these play-in games to trim the field to the traditional tournament size of eight teams, while the losers of the play-in games play each other to ensure each team plays at least two games in the tournament. Needless to say, we really wanted to get into the eight-team quarterfinal round of the bracket. A loss in the play-in game would end our chances to accomplish anything in the tournament nearly before the tournament began.

Our game with North Harrison was played the Saturday before the week of the tournament, which was hosted by Winston. We started the game on a roll, and sustained it throughout the game. North Harrison had some fast players, but we played a tight diamond and one press, which led to several turnovers and fast break layups for us. Since I was the "one" in the press who stayed back to prevent an easy layup should the press be broken, I spent much of the first half watching my teammates steal the ball and get quick layups. Our press was working about as well as it would at any time that season, allowing us score an avalanche of points in transition. Once we really got to running and pressing, we were able to rout a decent team.

We also played good half-court zone defense, rotating to close lanes for driving and passing. When one of us would pull down a rebound, we threw a quick outlet pass and started another fast break. With our offense scoring points in a hurry and our defense suffocating the Shamrock attack, we cruised to a 60-21 win. We played a very good team game, helping each other out and not relying on one or two players to carry the team. The win lifted us to 6-12 on the season and gave us momentum heading into our next game in the HDC Tournament, a matchup with North Mercer, one of the HDC's best teams.

Mercer's teams played with a machine-like efficiency, running offensive sets to near perfection until a good scoring opportunity arrived. They were confident teams, due largely to their success. However, we had won four of our last six games and two in a row, so we were confident about our chances to pull the big upset.

In the first half, we came out in a 1-2-2 "matchup" zone to try to limit Mercer's capable outside shooters while still defending the post because of Mercer's post threat, Zack Martin. Martin wasn't very tall for a post player, but he thrived in the post due to his footwork, hustle, and strength. In our 1-2-2, the two bottom defenders could work together to control the post while the top three players could handle the perimeter. If everybody rotated and helped out while winning the matchups in their area, it was a very effective defense.

Kaleb and I were the two defenders on the blocks in the zone. Because I was a lot taller than Martin, he didn't really try to shoot on my side of the zone. However, Martin would cut across the lane, usually off a pick, and set up shop on Kaleb's side. Martin, a senior, would use head fakes and power to muscle in points for Mercer. Kaleb got in some foul trouble, which always makes it harder to defend. When I finally got it in my sophomoric mind to get over to the other side of the lane quicker and help out with a double team, we were able to limit Martin's post scoring. Kaleb and I also got some scoring going in the post. I had a good shooting night and was able to get good position to be effective in the post. I finished with 14 points and 10 rebounds, a good performance on the big stage of the HDC Tournament.

Mercer had built a small lead in the first half but couldn't put the knockout punch on us. They had three-point shooters very capable of nailing big treys, such as vaunted junior Jeff Girdner, but we were resilient, hustling at both ends of the court. One of us kept hitting a big shot just when it was critical for us to get one.

With a few seconds left in the third quarter, Mercer led Gilman City by nine points. Mercer had the ball and was looking to get the lead to double-digits heading into the fourth quarter. In a timeout, Coach Burke had us match up in man-to-man defense for the last play of the third quarter. Because I had played solid defense on Martin in the post, Burke had me guard Martin.

Unfortunately, Martin headed beyond the perimeter, where the advantage was his. Still, I was on him, all over him, don't let him score, can't let my guy score, then a pick and suddenly he was gone into the corner. Like a person chasing a loose paper in a strong wind, I frantically ran after him. Martin caught the ball in the corner and let fly a three. I futilely waved at the ball as it sailed over my head and swished through the net at the buzzer. That was embarrassing. Martin's rare trey put Mercer up by 12 going into the final period.

Despite that setback, we again showed our resilience by refusing to let this potential dagger bury us. We came out in the final period and made an improbable charge. We trimmed Mercer's lead to three with just under four minutes to go. With the momentum on our side, the crowd sensed a huge upset. If not on the ropes, we had Mercer near the ropes. Regrettably, three points was as close as we would get. Mercer didn't let the upset bid rattle them, and they played well down the stretch, while we didn't quite make the one or two big plays we needed to put us over the top. Often times in basketball games, one or two big plays at a critical point will change the entire complexion of the game, but we didn't get any of those plays. Mercer got some late free throws and the final score was Mercer 50, Gilman City 42. We played a good game and were proud of our effort, but were frustrated that we had come up just short. Our near-win had impressed those watching, providing a glimpse of what we could do in the future.

The loss put us in the loser's bracket, but we could still win the consolation trophy if we won our next two games. However, a loss in our next game, against tournament-host Winston, would be the end of our tournament.

We had defeated Winston by 27 points earlier in the season, but the Redbirds had greatly improved as the season went along. Winston had a young team that was moving toward the top of the conference. For the rest of my high school years, Winston and Gilman

City would have very evenly-matched boys' basketball teams. Gilman City faced Winston nine times when I played, and seven of the last eight meetings were decided by eight points or less.

Winston's Eric Lewis was a good coach who always seemed to get the most out of his players, regardless of what their talent level was. He was also good at making adjustments. After my 18-point performance against Winston earlier in the year, Lewis had his team run a 2-1-2 defense with defenders behind and in front of any of us that tried to post up. This limited our advantage near the basket, where we had more tall players than Winston, such as Kaleb, Tony, and myself. It was also tougher to drive into the lane with it clogged with defenders, slowing down our players who were adept at driving to the hoop, such as Jacob and Sawyer.

The zone forced us to rely more on our outside shooting, which wasn't good for a team that shot 21% on threes for the year. As the game went on, we found ways to step up our scoring, such as fast breaks. We also got to working the ball around more in the half-court offense, which eventually led to breakdowns and openings in Winston's zone defense. Winston also ran a press against us, which required us to remain patient and focused to break. Again, patience and focus aren't usually very prevalent in high school boys, but we did fairly well with them once we got settled down.

Despite our ball movement and ability to break the press usually, Winston held on to a narrow lead throughout the fourth quarter. Our offense got rolling, with several players contributing points, but we couldn't come up with enough defensive stops late in the game to catch the Redbirds. Winston's point guard, Cody Lang, made several key plays in the second half for his team. He would often drive into the lane and quickly loft a shot over my outstretched arms or dish it off to an open teammate when our defense collapsed on him. I was one of the tallest players in the area and could block a lot of shots, but it was always very difficult to block one of Lang's shots. He was quick and made good decisions as to what he could do in the lane.

Winston held their lead and won by a score of 74-66. The loss put us out of the tournament and dropped our season record to 6-14.

Despite only winning one of our three tournament games, we were encouraged by our narrow losses to two quality teams, although it was annoying to come up short in both. We had had good opportunities to make a big splash on the stage of the HDC Tournament, but they had slipped away.

Our first game after the tournament was at North Mercer, which gave us an opportunity to score the upset we had nearly accomplished the week before. Unfortunately, the game was not so close this time. Nothing seemed to go right for us as Mercer sprinted to an early lead. We came out flat and stayed that way for most of the game, making for a very disappointing performance. Mercer won the blowout game by a score of 76-45. The only noteworthy thing about the game came when Mercer's junior guard Jeff Girdner scored his 1,000th point in the game. Other than that, it was just another bad loss for us, our third loss in a row. We were now 6-15 on the season.

In contrast to the bad loss was our next game, at Ridgeway, a game we thought we should win. Although Ridgeway had some good shooters and basketball players, we had beaten them in a close game in the Gilman Tournament, and we were eager to prove we were a better team than 6-15. Ridgeway ran a press, but we were very effective at breaking it and scoring fast break points when one of us slipped behind the defense for an open layup. Ridgeway often pressed us. Oddly, sometimes we broke it fairly easily and sometimes it caused us to make multiple turnovers. I think a lot of the difference in our ability to break their press lay in our approach to getting the ball up the court. Passing and patience were very important for us to break a press. We had some good athletes, but it came down to our decision-making.

We made the right decisions on this night. In a complete reversal of our previous game with Mercer, we won a blowout game, 76-52. I bounced back from a poor game against Mercer to have a very good one on this night, finishing with 17 points, 13 rebounds, and three blocks. Kaleb also had a great game, getting a double-double in points and rebounds. Between our good offensive nights and a low-mistake effort from the rest of the team, we equaled our highest offensive output of the year with 76 points. It was great for our confidence after losing three in a row. The win also lifted our conference record to a respectable 3-4.

Next up for us were our last two home games, one road game, and then Districts. The season had hit the homestretch. The first of the two home games was with North Harrison. We had beaten them by 39 points in the HDC Tournament, but we were a very up-and-down team, and North Harrison had played below their normal level of play in our previous meeting. Perhaps our youth and inexperience led to our inconsistency. However, it was late enough in the season inexperience really shouldn't be an excuse anymore. Despite the large margin of victory in our previous matchup with North Harrison, this game was a close, tightly contested battle.

We couldn't score at nearly the rate we did in the earlier game as the Shamrocks limited our fast breaks. I was particularly absent on offense, scoring only four points on a pathetic 2-for-10 shooting performance. It was the lowest scoring output of my high school career. Late in the game, with our team needing scoring desperately, no one really stepped up. It was incredibly frustrating in the fourth quarter as the game slowly slipped away. We had a lead, but as we answered Shamrock baskets with misses, the lead melted into a deficit. It was an agonizing feeling, as we seemed powerless to save the game. North Harrison won the game 50-44. In the final seconds of the game, when it had become apparent we would lose, I stood near half court after a foul call and my thought was: how could we have blown this game? We beat this team by 39 points less than a month ago! But we had lost it, or North Harrison had taken it from us, or both.

It was a down point in the season, but we had a chance to end the home schedule on a high note with our senior night game against Winston. It was also our last regular season HDC game.

One of our seniors, Tony, tried before the game to get Heath to shave a "55" in the back of his head. (55 was Tony's number.) Now Heath was willing to do some crazy things if persuaded properly, such as our senior year Homecoming skit when he punctuated his dance sequence by pulling off his shirt, so, after some pre-game barber work, Heath ran out on the court with a semi-readable "55" in the back of his head. I always liked running out on the court before games. The fans are cheering you, the potential of the game lies ahead of you, and the running and subsequent layup drills calm any nerves I ever had before games.

The game was the rubber match of the Gilman City-Winston season series, which was tied at one win apiece after our meetings in tournaments. Perhaps it was the extra intensity produced by playing our last home game of the season, but we jumped out to an early lead. After struggling to keep up in our previous game with Winston, it was our turn to control the game.

Since he was a senior and we had a lead, Tony played more than he normally did. He was a good role player, coming in sometimes to play alongside me in the post or to give me a break. When Tony and I were both in the game, we anchored the post part of our zone defense. We could each take more chances on blocks because we knew there would be another big player backing us up. Despite playing good defense, Tony's senior night highlight came when he pulled up with the ball on a fast break and inexplicably let fly a three, his only attempt from beyond the arc of the season. I hustled to the block in position for what everyone thought would be the inevitable rebound only to watch as the ball bounced on the rim a few times and went in. It was one of many things to go our way as we won, 59-46. It was a solid team effort, with our defense holding our opponent in the 40s while our offense scored nearly 60 points. The win lifted our overall record to 8-16, a nice recovery after a 2-10 start. We finished the conference schedule with a 4-5 record, a decent foundation to build on next year.

We had one more regular season game before the district tournament, a nonconference contest at Osborn. With snow beginning to fall, we loaded on the bus and headed south to Osborn. The late-February snow melted some as it hit the ground, so it didn't really affect travel. It was just another bus ride, the trip interrupted only when the big yellow bus hit one of the cracks and divots on I-35. The resulting bump occasionally sent players and gym bags flying through the air.

Upon arrival, we put our stuff in our "locker room," which was an elementary classroom near the gym. We sometimes had a classroom as our locker room on the road, as it was a common thing for area schools to have visiting teams change in a classroom near the gym. (Except at Albany, which had us change in what appeared to be the football locker room, situated roughly 17.4 miles from the gym.) It wasn't a problem at all to change in a classroom, except for one small issue. When you wanted to sit down in an elementary classroom, there were only small seats built for little kids. The only normal-sized chair was the teacher's chair, which Coach Burke appropriately sat in.

After putting our stuff in the locker room, we went to watch the Gilman girls team play the Osborn Lady Wildcats. We cheered for the Lady Hawks with the Gilman fans while some members of our team scouted the Osborn girls team for "prospects." The game was close, but our girls eventually lost by nine.

By this point of the season our preparations were very routine. We went to our dressing room at the end of the third quarter of the girls' game. After we stretched and dressed, Coach Burke came in to talk about the game and our strategy for a few minutes before we went out on the court to do warm up drills and shoot before the game.

Our game with Osborn was fast-paced from the opening tip-off. Osborn had a small team, but the pushed the ball up the court as quickly as possible and ran a press to cause turnovers and speed up the game's tempo.

We also had some team speed, and I had a size advantage in the post, but their press and our bad defense really hurt our chances to win. Horrendous is probably a more accurate word to describe our defense on that night. Osborn would blow by us like we were folding chairs for layups or find alarmingly open threes on the perimeter. We scored a good amount of points that night, but we gave up far too many to have a realistic chance to win. We lost 95-62.

Osborn had tried to score 100 on us by pressing very late into the fourth quarter and constantly pushing the ball up the court despite a 30-point lead. It seemed like retaliation from the year before, when Gilman beat Osborn in a blowout. Gilman's eight seniors had dominated Osborn in their last home game and some Osborn people thought Gilman was trying to run up the score. I think both years were mostly a case of a better team playing very well on their respective senior nights, but the two routs caused a little animosity between the schools for a couple years. Matters were not helped when the parent of an Osborn player yelled at Kaleb in a poor attempt to heckle. In most games I played in, fans didn't yell at players on the other team. They yelled at refs and players on their own team (usually their children) and muttered complaints about other players among themselves. Once in a while, when we played bigger GRC schools, students from their schools would sit together and yell stuff. I kind of liked this because it added to the game atmosphere. However, a parent yelling at a kid on the other team during a 30-point blowout is kind of pathetic. He must have forgotten why he was there, which was presumably to watch his son. Overall, the usual lack of heckling and the fact nobody was making money off our games were big reasons our games seemed fun and pure.

These contentious feelings seemed to be isolated incidents, however, because my junior and senior games with Osborn were regular games, devoid of anything controversial.

I had a decent game despite our bad loss, with 21 points and nine rebounds. I could score a lot in the post and on fast breaks when we broke their press, but Osborn simply scored more than any of us could. After the game, an Osborn fan told me I'd played a good game. It was a nice gesture, a good example of sportsmanship. I liked fans that cheered hard for their team but still recognized good basketball performances. It was probably easier for their fans to be gracious to us, however, since we lost badly.

There wasn't time for us to be down on ourselves, however, because next week was the District Tournament. The District Tournament is the most important part of the schedule. The schedule is full of rivalry games, Homecoming, and other tournaments, but Districts stand out. They are the start of the state playoffs. Before the first year I played, the playoffs were restructured, putting Gilman City in the eight-team Class 1 District 14 Tournament. Three wins make a team the District Champions. The District winner goes to the sectional "Sweet 16" game in Chillicothe. The winner of that game plays in the state quarterfinal game in Maryville. The winner of that game plays in the Class 1 Final Four at Mizzou Arena in Columbia, which Gilman City has reached three times. The state playoffs are wonderful for its simple, step-by-step style. Teams go from Districts to Chillicothe to Maryville to Columbia. Starting at Districts, five wins are needed to earn a final four berth, with seven wins resulting in a state championship. What gives the tournament its drama is that one loss ends a team's season. It's fascinating to see how underclassmen handle the added pressure of Districts or to watch seniors frantically fight off the end of their careers.

Our District was full of good teams, especially on the girls' side. In fact, the No. 1 and No. 2 girls Class 1 teams in the state, North Mercer and Worth County, were seeded to meet in the District 14 championship game. In the boys' bracket, we had our third matchup of the season with Ridgeway in the first round.

We had beaten Ridgeway twice that year, but it's often said it's hard to beat a team three times in a year. That's especially true when your season win total heading into Districts is eight. Also, we knew Ridgeway could score a lot of points and the game was seeded to be close since we were a No. 4 seed and they were a No. 5 seed. With Levi Price, Aaron Fitzpatrick, and a few other solid supporting players, the Owls could be a difficult team to beat.

The District Tournament was in Eagleville that year, hosted by the North Harrison High School. Prior to the game, Coach Burke stressed that it was important to establish our post game because we had an advantage there and it would open up our outside game.

We came out and did just that. On one of our first possessions I got the ball in the post. I felt the defender on my left shoulder, playing me to turn left for a hook shot or right-handed layup, so I pivoted to my right and made a short jumper. Feeling out the defenders instead of just making a random move was one way I had improved as a post player in my first season.

We attacked the post early, controlling the game's tempo. Our game plan was working. In a season when our offensive production was up and down, this was a game in which our offense was up. I contributed 19 points to our high-scoring performance, which resulted in a 79-62 win. The 79 points were the most we scored in a game all season. We also played much better defense than in the game with Osborn. I had a very powerful block when one of Ridgeway's guards tried to drive to the hoop on a fast break. Blocks always seemed to give me extra energy on the court. I loved the feel of a clean block, particularly when it came at the expense of a guard who had ventured into the lane.

The win set up a second-round matchup with the North Mercer Cardinals, the District's top seed. Mercer had beaten us twice that year. Also, Mercer had several players who had been on District-winning teams from the past few years, while Jacob was our only player with meaningful District experience prior to that season.

After our first-round win and upsets earlier in the season, we felt we had a good chance to knock off the No. 1 seed on the biggest stage we'd ever played on, Districts.

In the first half, Mercer had a lead, but we stayed within striking distance, as we had against Mercer in the HDC Tournament. I started out as a powerful post presence, overcoming Mercer's physical defense to make most of my shots, which caused Mercer's coach to yell, "Watch Herrold!" on inbounds plays.

A developing problem for us in the game was our lack of depth. Our seniors, Tony and Darrin, had left the team for various reasons late in the season, leaving us with only seven players for Districts. Junior Daniel Prindle was sick before the Mercer game and couldn't come, leaving us with only six players, just one player on the bench at a time. This wasn't a problem of stamina or endurance, because many of us starters played most of the game regardless of how many subs were available. I wanted to be on the court as much as possible, obviously, and often played the entire game. Playing the entire game wasn't a problem for most of us this late in the season; we were in great shape from all the running during the season. The problem with only having six players was foul trouble. A few of our players picked up early fouls, but only one could sit out at a time. The others in foul trouble had to play conservatively to avoid getting more fouls. With more people playing with fouls, more of our players fouled out.

The game, which was reasonably competitive in the first half, turned into an ugly rout in the second half. Early in the fourth quarter, we began to have players foul out and Mercer began to pull away. When our second player fouled out, we had to play with four. The game got out of hand and Mercer stalled the ball with several minutes to go. I guess it was good sportsmanship not to run it up on an undermanned team, but we wanted to spend the last few minutes of our season playing basketball, not standing around. We played tight defense to get the ball back a few times, creating some nice turnovers. We had another player foul out late in the game, adding to the frustration of it all. When the game finally ended, Mercer had won 64-26 as Matt, Kaleb, and Sawyer had fouled out, which left Heath, Jacob and I to play the last few minutes three on five. It was an embarrassing, ugly way to end our season. It was bad enough kids from other schools would ask me what it's like to play three on five for almost a year after the game, but it was also bad the margin of victory had been so outlandish. We lost by 38 points, our third loss of the year to Mercer.

Our season was over, but a group of us came back to Eagleville the following night to watch the District Championship games. We thought we could make the District Championship game next year, and we wanted a fresh memory of what it was like. Also, both the girls' and boys' title games featured intriguing matchups between North Mercer and Worth County, a GRC school that was small enough to be Class 1. The girls' game featured the No. 1 and No. 2 Class 1 teams in the state. We wanted to see the top teams face off, and District Championship games are almost always exciting, intense games.

The girls' game was an epic, featuring a battle between the HDC and GRC champions. The Mercer girls had dominated the HDC for the last four years, the duration of the careers of a group of seniors. Those senior girls had lost one regular season HDC game in their careers. They had led Mercer to three straight District titles and had reached the state quarterfinals the last couple of years. This year they were aiming for a Final Four berth.

The realignment before the season had put the Worth County Tigers into the Class 1 Tournament and into Mercer's District. Worth County had come through the rugged GRC with games against tough teams like South Harrison, Hamilton, and Gallatin. Worth County countered Mercer's All-State guard tandem of Hannah Stark and Lauren Wilson with April Miller, one of the state's best point guards. The Tigers also had Charlea Lewis in the post, a massive, dominating low post scorer. Mercer's post defenders had some height and lots of experience, but they were skinny, which made it difficult to handle Charlea in the paint. Both teams had steady supporting casts, which added to the overall quality of the game.

When we arrived at the game, the gym was so full we had to stand at the corner of the gym that led to a locker room. North Harrison's gym is one of the biggest in the HDC, so a packed house there is a crowd of considerable size.

Neither team could pull away as the two best teams in the state battled it out. Charlea went to work in the post, which Stark and Wilson countered with their stellar outside shooting. Late in the game, with Worth County clinging to a narrow lead and the pressure at its highest, Miller stayed steady, running the offense almost flawlessly without making mistakes. The brilliant play by the guards in the game was an example of senior leadership. In the end, Worth County won and moved on to the state playoffs, ending the illustrious careers of the Mercer seniors. As the Worth County players celebrated wildly on the court, the Mercer girls filed past us to their locker room, tears running lines through their makeup. The spectrum of emotions displayed was staggering, as happens in big sports games with the inevitable winners and losers. The Worth County girls would go on to the Final Four that year.

The boys' game, although it wasn't a No. 1 versus No. 2 situation, featured two very good teams. The Mercer boys were every bit as efficient as they were against us. Although Mercer had beat us three times that year, I kind of wanted them to win because they were representing the HDC against the GRC. Also, the farther they went, the better we would look. Mercer started well, as they usually did. Despite several valiant rally attempts by Worth County in the second half, Mercer held on for the win.

After the game, Kaleb, Seth, Zack, and I went to the Dinner Bell. After the excitement of the District Championship games, Kaleb and I wanted to experience them as a player. When someone pointed out the Mercer boys would be good again next year, I quipped, "Maybe we'll get the two seed and won't have to worry about them until the championship game."

It would all have to wait until next year, because our 2002-03 season was over. We finished the year with a record of 9-18. That wasn't very impressive, but we had improved drastically as the season progressed, going a respectable 4-5 in conference play. Also, we had scored a big upset over our rival Tri-County and took second in the Gilman Tournament. We had also acquired valuable experience playing high school basketball, laying the foundation for next year. There was plenty for us to build on. However, we had lost two games for every one we won. We would have to improve on that next year.

Several of us had improved a lot as individual players. I learned the nuances of playing the post at the high school level and established myself as a reliable post scorer and rebounder. I had scored 326 points, averaging a solid 12.1 points per game. I made 50% of my shots, which I felt was important because anyone could score if they shot all the time. I had also averaged 8.3 rebounds and 1.6 blocks per game. All of these led our young team. I was also named

HDC All-Conference Honorable Mention. I had become a leader on the team, a player who could help the team in a variety of ways. Still, I wanted to get a lot better. I wanted to be a better outside shooter, to be more consistent, and most of all to be able to help lift the team to more wins. Nine a year isn't enough.

Jacob Webb had also been HDC All-Conference Honorable Mention. He had provided vocal leadership and had scored 10.8 points per game. Kaleb had also shown he could contribute a lot to our offense, scoring 9.0 points per game. Sawyer, Heath, Matt, and Daniel were all much better players than when the season had begun.

With all of our key players back for my junior season, we had the pieces in place to achieve a lot. There were optimism and anticipation about the next season. The 2003-04 season lay ahead, with its achievements and memories ready to be claimed.

CHAPTER 6

My junior season, 2003-2004, would be a memorable one for a variety of reasons, some good and some bad. It would be the ultimate example of a roller coaster season, with high drama and lasting accomplishments. The season was a whirlwind of achievements, letdowns, and challenges, each constantly parading past our team and saturating us with experience.

The season began with high expectations for our team. We had all our significant contributors back from the previous season. After laying the foundation during my sophomore year, this was the year to be winners, to bring home trophies and the pride that comes with them.

Our 2003-04 team had four seniors, Jacob Webb, Matt Houser, Daniel Prindle, and Chad Cole, who was the only one of the four who hadn't played the year before. The four of us from my class, Kaleb, Heath, Sawyer, and I, were playing as juniors this year. We also got some new players in sophomores Jarett Webb and Daniel Dennert as well as freshman Kyle King. We had a lot of team speed with players like Sawyer, Kaleb, Matt, and Jacob. They could cut or drive to the hoop and were now able to elevate and hit shots around the hoop, which we couldn't do consistently the year before. With myself at center and Sawyer and Kaleb as forwards, we also had some very good post players. Heath and Jacob were both solid 3-point threats by this season. After a year of playing together, we had pretty good team defense.

I had high hopes for our team that year, and I wanted to become more of a team leader. I wasn't really a vocal leader because I wasn't really a vocal person, but I wanted to lead by example and make the team better overall with the way I played. During my sophomore year I had established myself as one of our team's solid contributors but I wanted to step up my level of play to another, more dominating level. Simply put, I wanted to be the best post player in the conference. I worked a lot on basketball over the summer by shooting or playing games, and I worked a lot to improve my hook shot and to add the 15-18 foot jump shot to my game. I wanted to become a great high school basketball player on a winning team.

This was the year, the time for any and all of our goals, even the absurd ones, to come true. We had an excellent chance to win the HDC title, to win some tournaments, or to play in one of those intense, mythical District Championship games. The pieces were in place; we were ready.

Unfortunately, an incident the summer before the season shook up our roster. It was during the Gilman City Fair, in mid-July. The fair was a change of pace from routine summer activities like working on the farm and summer basketball. It was a classic evening at the Gilman City Fair, the town's midsummer classic. It had been a very hot day, with big fans running in the livestock area in an effort to keep the show livestock comfortable. After the long day of oppressive heat the summer evening was settling in, cooling things off. People milled about, conversing and eating barbecue from the FFA food stand. Others walked over to the livestock showing area, carrying Styrofoam cups of lemonade or cans of Mt. Dew. The FFA adviser, some fair volunteers, and some of the FFA chapter officers were at a table next to the show ring, working the show. Shining trophies and paperwork lay on the table. I was the FFA reporter for two years in high school, which meant I was usually one of those officers at the table. My job was primarily to take pictures of the trophy-winning livestock and the people who showed them. Trying to get the a livestock exhibitor, fair board member, and bull to all hold a pose for a picture can be tricky, especially given my mediocre photography skills. Behind the show ring, girls and guys showing livestock walked around with brushes and ribbons sticking out their back pockets, getting their animals ready to be inspected by the judge. Multiple livestock trailers were parked around the livestock barn. Members of the community sat on the bleachers around the show ring, enjoying the evening. A talent show took place on the other side of the food stand, which was selling homemade ice cream. The brick massiveness of the school and the great grain bins of the elevator framed the scene. The sunset was a brilliant orange and red painting on the huge canvas of the western sky. It was one of those evenings that could make one fall in love with Gilman City.

Because I was in FFA, I helped out at the fair, either at the show ring or in the food stand. It was while I was taking orders in the food stand that I heard the news. Jacob Webb had hurt his ankle playing basketball on the school tennis courts. This was a somewhat odd injury, as Jacob rarely played at the tennis courts during the summer and wasn't even on any summer league basketball teams. People said the ankle was hurt badly but nobody really knew exactly what the injury was. I'm always a little cautious when I hear news by word of mouth in Gilman because people in the community like to visit and give the news while sometimes deviating from the truth on details, either intentionally or unintentionally. Occasionally rumors and even rumors about rumors make the rounds in the conversations around town, and they are often exaggerated or inaccurate.

This time, however, the reports were true. Jacob had torn ligaments in his foot. No bones had been broken, but that may have made things worse because lots of things in his foot were tore up as the bones held their shape during the injury.

The injury would keep him from practicing until around Christmas break. He played one game in the early-season Gallatin Invitational Tournament but then decided to rest the ankle until our conference games started, to be safe. The rest of us on the team had the opportunity or the obligation to step up and fill the void while he was out, depending on your perspective. Either way, we would face our rugged nonconference schedule without our second highest scorer from the year before and our most experienced player.

Our first game was at Princeton, a GRC school. With Princeton again making a deep run in the state football playoffs, a few of their players wouldn't be playing in the game. Despite missing a few of their players, Princeton still fielded a very competitive team with some athletic guards and a big post player.

It was played like the first game of the season, with players picking up a lot of fouls, running wrong routes on inbounds plays, and generally playing rusty. Wanting to start the season in the best possible way, I was pressing a little early in the game, trying to force things that weren't there. Being a tall player, I could almost always elevate and get off a reasonable shot, but this wasn't always the best shot our team could get. I also missed a few shots early on that I should have made. Soon enough, I got going, earning trips to the foul line to get started. As the game went on we played better, building about a 10-point lead. Our offense began to have some flow to it, with good ball movement and quality shots. I played better as well, turning in the good, all-around performance my team needed from me. Besides scoring points for the team, I also picked up a lot of rebounds and blocks to help anchor the defense. I finished with 16 points, 11 rebounds, and five blocks, a good way to start the season. It was the kind of all-around game I wanted to have, because my team needed more than just points from me for us to win. Several players on our team could score some points, but each of us had other specialties to contribute to the team, be it rebounding, passing, ball handling, defense, or a combination of these.

We were very steady down the stretch, protecting our lead despite spirited Princeton rallies and some foul trouble for us. I was usually good about avoiding foul trouble, as I only fouled out of one game in my career, so I was able to play the entire game since I didn't have very many fouls. When the game ended, we had played well enough to earn a 59-50 victory to start our season. We were 1-0 and now even more excited about the rest of the season.

We looked to build on the win in the Gallatin Invitational Tournament. The GIT is sort of a de facto season opener tournament; a barometer of how a team is playing to start the season. Also, the program for the GIT has a season preview with a few paragraphs about each GRC and HDC team. There's anticipation for the season ahead hanging over the games. Fans get an idea of what they will be watching all winter, although these early games can paint an inaccurate picture of the season ahead because high school teams can greatly improve or falter over the course of an entire season. There are feelings of optimism for most teams, and the program's season preview reflects that optimism.

For whatever reason, it's fun to have your name in the paper for a performance in a game or in a season preview. It's nice to have your work recognized and for people in the area to hear about your achievements. Newspaper clips are something for parents and grandparents to read and save, something to remember your basketball experience with. It is one of sport's allures beyond just the competition and fun: doing something newsworthy, something that seems to be lasting that other people notice and that you can be proud of.

We again faced a difficult first-round opponent in the GIT, the 3A Hamilton Hornets. Hamilton had a very good team that year. We could continue to build our confidence and the excitement around the team by just playing a good game against one of the toughest opponents on our schedule. Instead, the game was a terrible performance for us, and we lost 70-37. We had a chance to make some noise in a big-time tournament and we had met with disaster seemingly before our week had begun. The game doesn't really merit much comment. Although Hamilton was a very good team, we had no excuse to lose that badly, not this year. The 33-point loss was frustrating, an annoying piece of evidence that suggested we hadn't come that far from the previous year, when our young team lost four of our first six games by 30 points or more. We were very eager to put the game out of our minds and move on.

There were still games to be played in the tournament and things to play for, such as the consolation trophy two wins would bring. The only positive coming from the loss to Hamilton was it set up a losers' bracket match for us with Tri-County. Although the only thing on the line was a berth in the consolation (5th place) game, it was still an intense battle between two rivals. We bounced back from our bad loss to Hamilton with a tremendous effort against the Mustangs. It was a tight, intense, draining contest throughout, but we pulled out a 61-56 win. The win gave us back-to-back wins over Tri-County. I was starting to be known for big games against the Mustangs after our win last year, and I made an impact in this game as well, scoring 18 points on 9-of-14 shooting. I also pulled down 11 rebounds. This combined with great rebounding efforts by Sawyer and Kaleb to help us hang onto the game in the second half. It usually seemed like our individual rebounding performances fed off each other, probably because the zone defense we usually played relied on each person boxing out his area for the others to rebound effectively.

The victory launched us into our consolation match with Winston at 2-1 on the season. Winston presented a difficult challenge. They were a good, fundamentally sound team with excellent team defense. They usually played a tight, collapsing zone defense that made rebounding and post scoring difficult, which happened to be two of my primary contributions to the team.

It was another tightly contested Gilman City-Winston game. Our previous close battles added to the intensity of the game, as did the consolation trophy that was on the line. In sports, there is a sharp contrast between the winners and the losers. This contrast was sharpened in this game by the difference between going 2-1 in the GIT and earning a trophy and going 1-2 in the tournament and wondering what happened.

I remember our team playing so hard in the game, almost frantically trying to build a lead on the Redbirds. My performance in the game was long on effort but short on results on the offensive end. For instance, I pulled down 11 rebounds but only scored eight points. I was just off my game most of the night, one of those games when you just inexplicably play much worse than you normally do. On one fast break, I didn't time my steps right and blew a lightly contested layup. When I handled the ball, I seemed to be playing with boxing gloves on. Despite having an off night, I occasionally broke through the fog to hit a shot or win a battle for a rebound. On nights like this I had to stay confident and keep hustling and not dwell on missed shots or turnovers. On a night when a lot of our players were having unsteady games, Heath provided steady play. He provided quality ball handling in the face of Winston's press and hit two big threes at critical points in the close contest. Jacob also helped break the press as he played one game to test his ankle. He would later decide to rest it and not play in any more games until after Christmas break. Sawyer led our offense that night, scoring 13 points. His athleticism lifted our team on a night when our offense was struggling a little.

Late in the game, we trailed by one with under 20 seconds to play, due largely to a big three-pointer for Winston late in the game. Coach Burke called a timeout, setting up a play in which Jacob had the ball with me in the post as an option for him to pass to. Jacob got the ball in the final seconds and he passed it to me in the post. I turned and launched a shot as I jumped with a second or two to go. The shot was for the game and the consolation trophy. I had made tons of these 8-12 foot shots before. I could be the hero, kind of like in the Tri-County game the year before. The ball hung in the air for what seemed to be a long time. The ball briefly, tantalizingly appeared to be going in, but it clanked off the rim and missed as the buzzer sounded. Winston 54, Gilman City 53. I had missed the game-winner. As the Winston players celebrated wildly, I walked over to the sideline and got in line for the post-game handshakes and "good-games."

Now I know one shot doesn't determine an entire game and many plays were responsible for us losing by one and all that stuff nice people tell players who miss game-winning shots, but I still felt terrible about missing that shot. I could have won the game, been the hero, and made up for a sub par performance, but instead we lost and I just highlighted a poor performance. In a way, that contrast, that impact of one big play, is one of the many reasons I love sports.

Coach Burke and my teammates were supportive after the game. Everybody was mostly upset we'd lost a winnable trophy game. Nobody played really well. We had all played a role in losing a game we could have won. Afterwards, as I walked out into the brisk winter evening, I saw Mr. Tibbles, a teacher at our school who also drove the bus to the games. He gave me a thumbs-up, a nice gesture of support without getting caught up in saying the "right thing." Sometimes words aren't required.

Fortunately, we were able to move on quickly from the burning loss because we had to focus on the upcoming games against Hamilton and at Gallatin. These are bigger schools, and they presented a good test for us.

The Hamilton game was a disaster, even worse than when we played them in the tournament. We lost 70-27, a 43-point train wreck of a loss. After thinking we were a good enough team to not get blown out any more, it was a very frustrating loss to say the least.

We continued our slide downhill against Gallatin, hitting rock bottom in a 67-22 loss. It was an egregious, crushing 45-point loss. That debacle left us at 2-4 on the season.

Our season, looking so promising after beating Tri-County, had took a downward turn with the frustrating loss to Winston. The two losses to Hamilton and Gallatin by a combined 88 points left us with a three-game losing streak. The bad losses were unnerving, but we knew our team could and should play a lot better. Besides, high school basketball seasons can be reborn with one good game that gets a team going. Despite our underwhelming start, our season still had a lot of potential. We were a bunch of optimistic teenagers, so we were still confident.

We did need to right the ship in a hurry, however, because our next game was our first conference game. At home against Pattonsburg, it was a game we should win. We were able to focus on the conference game and not worry about our previous losses, which didn't really matter a whole lot.

We gave the home crowd something to be proud of after the embarrassing home loss to Hamilton. We turned the tables to win a blowout game by a score of 52-21. Pattonsburg didn't have a great team that year, but the win ended our losing streak and gave us something to build on heading into Christmas break. We were 3-4 overall and 1-0 in HDC play going into the break.

Following the break, we had a week of two non-conference games before resuming conference play. The first was at Albany, followed by a home game with the Polo Panthers. Albany had a big, supportive crowd and, being a bigger school, they also had a fairly vocal student section. Gilman also had loud, supportive fans, even at a road games. There's always a good section of fans wearing blue and white in whatever gym Gilman is playing in. This made for a good game atmosphere. Unfortunately, we didn't play very well, despite our fans' cheers. Unable to score consistently, we lost 57-25. We hung around for a while with a decent defensive effort, but at some point you have to put the ball in the hoop to win. It was an annoying loss after so much work and practice over Christmas break. I had some offensive success in the post, scoring 12 points, but I couldn't do enough to lift the team with my play. Our team had a bad rebounding night, which gave Albany too many extra chances and shots.

We were now 3-5. We needed to string together some good performances to build some momentum after an inconsistent start to the season. We got started on this against Polo. We got revenge for last year's bad loss to Polo with a 60-33 win. We took the lead quickly and slowly pulled away, the opposite of what we did against Albany. I had one of my best games of the season, scoring 23 points on 10 of 16 shooting and pulling down 12 rebounds. It seems like a lot of the time that year an early shot or pass set the tone for how our game would go, for us as players and for the team as a whole. On this night, my first shot was a little awkward, arching higher than normal. But when it went in, it really seemed to get me going. Kaleb also had a good game, scoring 11 points and providing a variety of rebounds, assists, and steals.

The game built our confidence and gave us an opportunity to post back-to-back wins for the first time that year if we could win our next contest, our Homecoming game with Tri-County.

With the game being Homecoming and against our rival, there was a lot of buildup and anticipation before the game. The school was decorated with the traditional Homecoming displays. People around town were talking about the game. People who saw me around town always talked with me about basketball, and they all talked about beating Tri-County this week. Basketball was something people around town talked about, something that brought the town together, like planting in the spring and harvesting in the fall.

Even though Tri-County and Gilman City fans and players mostly got along well, there was always an intense desire on both sides to beat the other. Coach Burke talked about going to the Gilman City-Tri-County games as a kid and noticing how crazy everyone in the gym was going when the Hawks would be beating the Mustangs. The two schools usually designated the rivalry game as the Homecoming game for the home team when I played, adding to the intense game atmosphere. With back-to-back wins over the Mustangs, we were confident we had control of the rivalry. We stayed focused, however, because Tri-County had the players to do some damage. We knew our two wins over the Mustangs had been by a total of six points. Anything could happen in this rivalry, in which upsets were common. Tri-County's upset win at Gilman's Homecoming two years ago was a fresh memory for all of us.

Since our Homecoming theme was "Shake Ya Tailfethas" and our class was decorating a wall that had windows looking into the cafeteria, we decorated the wall like a nightclub. We spelled out "Club Shake Ya Tailfethas" in massive glittered letters at the top and put silhouettes of people in the windows, along with other decorations. The signature may have been the bouncer at the door, who was a bald guy with a goatee, drawn to be a Coach Burke look-alike. Kaleb and Krystal were our Homecoming king and queen candidates. A week of dressing up in crazy costumes culminated with blue and white day on Friday and an hour-long pep rally Friday afternoon. Friday night brought the actual game and an extra-packed house.

The Tri-County girls team won big over the Lady Hawks, but we sent the Homecoming crowd home with something to be happy about with our 62-48 win. We controlled the game throughout, winning without the drama of our win over Tri-County the previous year on our home court. We came out really fired up for the big game and grabbed and early lead, which we held on to throughout the game. We got outstanding performances from several players. Jacob had 17 points, Sawyer had a double-double in points and rebounds, and I added 14 points, six rebounds, and three blocks. With

Kaleb and Heath adding an array of points, rebounds, and steals, it was an impressive, balanced team effort.

We had come through in a big game. Homecoming coronation festivities are more enjoyable after a win. The win gave us three straight wins over the Mustangs and our first back-to-back wins of the year. We had improved to 5-5 on the season and 2-0 in HDC games. We had momentum heading into a week with three HDC road games that would go a long way toward determining our final HDC standing.

After the game, I was drenched with sweat and wore out from giving such effort in the game. We all were feeling great about the win, however. After Coach Burke's postgame speech, we joined the girls team in uniform in the corner of the gym, holding candles in anticipation for our role in the Homecoming ceremony. As we waited for some of the Homecoming candidates to make the transition from uniform to tuxedo, we talked about the game and made predictions as to who would be king and queen and wondered how long it took to put on a tuxedo. Soon enough, the lights were dimmed, the candles were lit, and the coronation tradition was carried out. After the ceremony we changed out of our uniforms. I put on my letter jacket and went out into the hall outside the gym, hearing congratulations and encouragement from Gilman fans. Later, as some other members of the Gilman student body were still showing their moves at the Homecoming dance, I stepped out into the clear, cold winter night, soaking up the memories of the night and enjoying the moment.

CHAPTER 7

One of the great discoveries for my class during our junior year of school was the ITV class. Gilman's school had a special room with eight TV's in it, four in the front and four in the back, as well as microphones and other technology used to teach. Other schools' ITV classrooms could be viewed on the TV's, and they could see us on their TV's. One teacher at a school could teach a class to kids at up to three other schools, with one TV showing what was going on at the teacher's home site. Most ITV classes were dual-credit, meaning a student could pick up high school and college credit for taking the class.

Besides the two-for-one deal on credit hours, ITV classes had many benefits not available in most regular classes at old GHS. One of these was that the ITV room was air conditioned, as it was a recently refurbished room. In the first and last months of the year, with many classrooms being without air conditioning, the school can get kind of hot. The ITV room is a refreshing alternative to the open-a-window cooling system in place in most of the school. While the school started putting in some window air conditioning units in a few classrooms in my final years there, most of the classrooms I was educated in had no air conditioning for most of my time there. We all survived without AC when we needed to, but the temperature-controlled ITV room was a nice change. The ITV room also had comfortable rolling chairs, which Mr. Tibbles used for some crazy Physics demonstrations when he taught the class in there. These chairs also enabled a few students to take an abbreviated nap during class.

Also, with the ITV system being relatively new, another "benefit" came when a school wouldn't be connected or would have technical difficulties, preventing class from being held that day. Also, with three or four high schools involved, there were more times when class can't be held because one of the schools had an assembly or trip. ITV classes also allowed us to visit with people from other schools and see what was going on there. It strengthened the connections between the schools in the area.

In one of my two ITV classes during my junior year, college algebra, I was the only person from Gilman taking the class. This meant I sat in the ITV room all alone and watched the teacher on TV from Pattonsburg. It was a little strange at first, but with my quiet personality type I was just fine sitting there for an hour and listening. The teacher, Sally Sparks, was very good at explaining things and working example problems so I got along real well learning through a TV.

My other ITV class that year was taught by Mr. Tolen, our principal at Gilman, so it was closer to being like a regular class. Also, the other people in my class were in there, so it was a more normal social environment, if you could call our class a normal social environment. There were also some girls from Eagleville who took the class, Mandy and Kimberly, who were on the North Harrison basketball team, so we talked about basketball and other stuff with them before and after class was going on.

There are, of course, lots of things to take students' focus off of academics. Some weeks this is the case more than others, such as the week in January when our team had three road games in five days. We had a rescheduled game on Monday at Cainsville, a Tuesday game at Newtown-Harris, and a Friday night game against traditional rival North Harrison on their Homecoming night.

It would be a rugged test, but our first opponent, Cainsville, was the weakest of the three teams we would face. Starting off the week with a win would give us three wins in a row, a winning record on the season, and momentum heading into the other road games.

A few hours after school on Monday, we loaded onto the bus and headed north to Cainsville, kicking off a week of great opportunity for our basketball team. At Cainsville, the visitor's locker room was a classroom. Since they generously selected a third-floor classroom, we got to pack our stuff up to the third floor, an invigorating pre-game warm-up.

After watching most of our girls team's reasonably close loss to Cainsville, we went upstairs to get ready to play.

Coach Burke came in to talk pregame strategy. It was mostly regular pregame instructions (push the ball up the court, run through the offense patiently until you get a good shot, etc.) with a few specific instructions (watch player X, try doing this differently against their 2-1-2 zone). He often drew up some of these instructions on the chalk board while us players finished stretching and tried to get rid of any pregame nerves. One difference in pregame instructions came when Coach told us we would be starting the game playing man-to-man defense instead of our usual zone. He wanted to see how we did playing man to see if we could use it later in the week and later in the season.

The man-to-man experiment didn't go so well. Our defense was ineffective early on as we allowed too many Cainsville players to get past us or get offensive rebounds. Our help defense was below average. I often had to go out on the perimeter to guard my man, taking me out of my usual role of guarding the lane. Cainsville hung around for a while as we struggled. Our man defense wasn't terrible, but it wasn't really good, either. We had the athletes to cover people, but we just didn't seem to shut down offenses in man like we could in zone defense. We were better guarding an area than a man, for whatever reason. Our rebounding also seemed better in zone defense. Our man defense would remain a work in progress.

When Coach Burke had seen enough and called for a 2-3 zone defense while sounding a little annoyed, we tightened the screws defensively. Our offense also came alive, turning the game into a rout. We pulled away to win 69-48. Several of us had big games in contributing to the win. I had a good start to the week, scoring 22 points on nine of 12 shooting and pulling down nine rebounds. The story of the night, however, was the play of sophomore Daniel Dennert. A reserve player, Daniel provided the highlight of the night. He once had the ball at the top of the key and shot a three. He buried it, drawing wild cheers from the crowd and the players on the bench. He added two made free throws to finish with a five-point night. After the game, everyone was talking about Daniel's big three.

The game gave us a good start to the week and a winning record on the season (6-5), but we had a quick turnaround with a game at Newtown the next night. The trip to Newtown was probably the longest for us of any HDC school we played, taking well over an hour. Also, I had started getting a cold on Monday. This sometimes happens to me in the winter, but I really hoped it wouldn't affect how I played during this week of important regular season games. I don't think it affected my play, but it was an inconvenience I could live without. When we boarded the bus to go to Newtown, my throat was kind of sore, and I couldn't really talk very much without my voice breaking up. Really, though, it wasn't anything that inhibited how I played, just how I talked. People who know me can attest there are probably no negative impacts on society if Benjamin Herrold can't talk very much.

The real drama as we waited to depart was the absence of Sawyer. He didn't show up, and we were wondering where else he could be that was more important than the bus to tonight's game. Newtown-Harris was a good team, and we needed all our players to succeed in the game. When it was time to leave, Sawyer still wasn't there. We had to leave for Newtown, assuming we would have to play without him. Finally, someone got in touch with him on a cell phone. It turned out he had overslept on a nap or something but would ride with his family to Newtown. Burke would sit him out for a quarter for missing the bus and then let him play. It was a relief to find out he was okay. It was also nice to know he could contribute to our effort that night.

There was an extra dimension to the game whenever I played against Newtown-Harris because my family had ties to the area. My parents lived in the area for about a decade until we moved to Nebraska. I was born when we lived there and was about 1 ½ years old when we moved to Nebraska. Although my family moved to Nebraska and then the Gilman City area, my parents have maintained friendships with a lot of people from Newtown. At games they catch up with their old friends. Before one of my sister Abbie's games at Newtown a sign in the town grocery store encouraged people to come to the game and see Dan Herrold.

It was when my parents lived on their farm near Newtown that my dad played town team basketball. After high school he played a couple years on the Spickard town team, then played for Newtown's town team for about a decade.

Town team basketball is woven in the tapestry of the region's heritage. It's not talked about a lot, but the marks of it are all over. Dad has really interesting stories to tell from his days playing and all the things he learned about basketball after playing all those years. He knows people from about every town that were on that town's team, and the old players are part of a subculture that watches out for each other and stays in touch.

Town team basketball was started after World War II by farm kids who didn't want to give up playing basketball after high school.

North Missouri is somewhat remote in places and this was something for people to do in the evenings. It thrived for decades up through around the time my family moved away. Dad's team played two or three times a week from around September to May, and NBA-like marathon schedule. Rough math with that schedule and playing for about 12-14 years would indicate my dad could have played over 1,000 town team basketball games. Each team had a contact guy to call to set up games. They played all over northern Missouri and southern Iowa. Because of all those years spent going all over to play games, my dad has a virtual north Missouri map in his head, knowing two or three different routes to towns I've never even heard of, as well as the alignment and location of businesses in dozens of towns all over the region.

The town teams would play at high school gyms, never canceling games due to weather. Once, Mom wondered with good reason about the feasibility of driving on icy roads into Newtown to play a game. Dad said, "Well, if the guys from Brookfield we're playing can make it up, I have to make it a few miles into town."

Around the late '80s, town team basketball kind of died out. The farm crisis in the '80s caused people to move off the farm and away from small towns. A new generation saw more people move away after high school or spend time at college. A unique era of the region's history came to an end, a part of society gone forever due to societal change.

I think this kind of basketball would have been fun to experience because it got to the heart of the game: the fun, competition, and camaraderie. From the '50s to the late '80s, town team basketball was a part of the small-town society in northern Missouri. Now it is only memories, memories personified in the former town team players who now watch their children play high school basketball.

Our game at Newtown meant a Herrold would again play basketball in the town. Also, it was a key HDC matchup as we were now

3-0 in conference games. Newtown-Harris was also contender for the HDC title. With players such as Nick Collins and Kyle Fordyce, Newtown had a very good offense. Fans came expecting a good game, and they were not disappointed.

A solid start gave us the early lead. I was on a roll to start the game. I was playing like the solid, at-times-dominant post player I had worked hard to become. Using hook shots, turnaround jumpers, and putbacks of errant shots, I took control of the post, that battleground of wills and effort. In the first half, I was even so bold as to launch a shot from 17 feet out. I had shot a lot over the summer in an attempt to extend my claustrophobic shooting range. When the ball splashed through the net and the Gilman fans cheered, it was validation for the work I'd done, a sign it was all worth the time and effort.

In the second half, with about a 10-point lead, we made sure to run our motion offense through again and again until we got a good shot. Once we went over 30 seconds before shooting. Kaleb and Sawyer were skilled at cutting to the basket both with the ball and to get open, and our patient running of the offense opened up lanes for them to do this.

Although our offense was running in high gear, Newtown would not go away. They were a resilient team, and they made a comeback, largely due to their good outside shooting. In a frenetic fourth quarter, with the clock running amazingly slow, our lead fell to three points with a few minutes to go. We showed some resilience of our own, refusing to cave in to the Newtown rally and their cheering home crowd. We hit enough big shots and free throws down the stretch to hold off the Newtown rally. With our late free throws, we pushed our final margin of victory to 68-56. The big win lifted us to 7-5 overall and an impressive 4-0 in conference play.

After the final seconds ticked off, we celebrated our fourth win in a row. After some early-season struggles, we had a chance for a special season. At 4-0, we had a great chance to win the HDC, which was one of our goals we talked about. An older Newtown fan, a friend of my parents, came out onto the court after the game and congratulated me for the game we'd just won. He said I'd played a heck of a game. I still couldn't talk very well with my sore throat, but I managed a "Thank You." I had 24 points and 12 rebounds in the game, one of the best performances in my career. To have one of my best games against a very good team in such a big game was awesome. Our season was beginning to live up to its potential.

On the radio on the way home we listened to the Missouri basketball team nearly beat highly ranked Texas. I'm a big Mizzou fan and I liked listening to Arthur Johnson play. I also was a fan of David Robinson, another member of the #50/post player club. I decided to wear #50 because of Robinson. I admired his ability as well as the class he displayed on the court, which I tried to emulate.

The two wins in two nights and four-game winning streak gave us lots of optimism heading into our Friday night game at North Harrison. It was the Shamrocks' Homecoming, so they would probably be fired up and drawing energy from their big crowd. We were focused in practice that week, the prospect of being 5-0 in conference being the carrot on a stick in front of us.

We talked some about the upcoming game with the North Harrison girls in ITV class. Every day they dressed up according to their Homecoming dress-up day, another reminder of the game looming at the end of the week. To the chagrin of some Gilman City boys, there was no Catholic schoolgirl dress-up day. Mandy and Kimberly had dressed up as Catholic schoolgirls on Halloween, although most of us had missed class that day for FFA National Convention or a field trip.

Friday, January 23 eventually came, bringing the game and my 17th birthday. After our third bus ride of the week came the games. We watched the North Harrison girls, a very good team that year, defeat our girls team, a rebuilding team, by over 30 points. It was then our turn to play.

The game was the basketball equivalent of walking into an ambush. North Harrison's massive old gym was filled with a Homecoming crowd that was buzzing in anticipation of the boys game to come and about the girls' big victory. Seconds after the tip, a normal basketball game was altered when North Harrison's Josh Smith drilled a three, drawing raucous cheers from the crowd. Had he missed that three, perhaps the game would have taken a different course. But Smith hit it, and that started a game-long barrage of threes for North Harrison. Smith was one of the Shamrocks' several good outside shooters and they all seemed to be hitting that night. With each three the crowd seemed to get louder and the North Harrison cheerleaders threw shirts into the crowd. The game was stuck in a pattern we couldn't seem to escape from: Gilman turnover or miss, North Harrison hits a three, shirts go flying into a roaring crowd. Where did they get so many shirts? How could cheerleaders have predicted this onslaught? The omnipresent, oversized green letters boomed "NHHS" on the wall of the gym. We were getting annihilated.

But we were no longer a team of starry-eyed first-year players. We had experience and enough talent and resolve to steady ourselves and make a run. We dug in on defense, crashing the boards to make sure the Shamrocks only got one shot. We overshifted our defense to focus on North Harrison's hottest shooters.

We cut down on the crippling turnovers that got us in trouble early in the game. We showed we could pour in points as well, and we slowly cut the deficit. I had a good game in the post on my birthday, scoring 22 points. I also hit six of seven free throws. I was able to score on them in the post, but I would often score two points on a post shot only to watch in disbelief as North Harrison buried another three. This was a frustrating exchange. We had some three-point threats of our own in Heath and Jacob, but we couldn't keep up with their outrageous shooting performance and intensity. We lost 68-60, our first conference loss of the season.

It's not real fun to lose, but we had simply been outplayed. Someone later told me North Harrison shot over 60% on three-pointers in the game, a fact easily backed up by my memories of the game. North Harrison was capable of playing way above their normal level that year, as they proved by their win over North Mercer that year.

We were now 7-6 with a 4-1 HDC record. The HDC regular season title was still very possible, despite our loss. That would wait for a week, however, as we now had the weeklong Gilman City Invitational Tournament.

My brother and dad had both won the Gilman Tournament, and I wanted to join the family tradition. Our team had made a surprising run to take second in the tournament the year before and we thought we could win the thing this year.

Our first-round opponent was the Worth County Tigers of the GRC. Worth County was a solid, physical team that presented a first-round challenge. It was a matchup of the No. 4 and No. 5 seeds, so it looked like it would be a good game. Before the game, Stewart Johnson, the KAAN radio broadcaster who was going to announce the game, asked me if I wanted to be called Ben or Benjamin on the air. Had I known he would ask, I might have thought of a creative or thoughtful answer. Instead I just said, "Either one's fine with me, whatever you want." I think he used Benjamin because that's what it was like in the program.

We played well against WoCo, winning 70-53 to move on the tournament semifinals. We played well by playing as a team, moving the ball around on offense and helping each other on defense. We featured a balanced scoring attack that night, with four players scoring in double figures. Jacob had 20 points, Kaleb had 15 points, Sawyer had 11 points, and I added 10 points. I also added 10 rebounds and eight blocks, a near triple-double.

For the second year in a row, we faced the tournament No. 1 seed in the semifinals of the Gilman tournament. This year it was the Princeton Tigers. We beat the Tigers earlier in the season, but they were without a few players who were still playing football. Now the football players were playing and Princeton had a big, physical team. It would be a challenge because they had some huge post players. As I've said, I am tall, but relatively skinny. I was about 6' 4", but I only weighed about 185 pounds. I would have to work hard to get position in the post. Our guards also faced a challenge in defending against Princeton's quick, athletic guards.

The game was close throughout, a back-and-forth battle. Our home crowd was in the game, giving us support, cheering for a win that would put Gilman City in the championship game of its tournament for the third year in a row.

Bret Cavanaugh, Princeton's primary post player, made it tough to post up very deep. I had to cut and slash and work very hard to get set up where I wanted to be, which was as close to the hoop as possible. When I did get set up, I was very effective, scoring 13 points on six-of-seven shooting. I was also just nimble enough to get open on the perimeter and hit an 18-foot jumper. Kaleb, Sawyer, and I worked together to keep Princeton's big men and leaping guards off the offensive rebounds. With a good display of team defense, we held Cavanaugh to eight points. After trailing by one at the half, we played a brilliant third quarter, outscoring Princeton 16-5 in the period. Our guards connected on some big threes to help us put away the Tigers. Heath hit two threes in the game and Jacob made three. Jacob led our offense with 19 points that night. We stayed strong down the stretch to win 56-47, somewhat atoning for our loss to Princeton in the Gilman tournament championship the year before. The next day the Trenton Republican-Times had a big picture of Sawyer flying through the air next to the story about the game, some nice media coverage to go with our win.

The win pushed our record to 9-6 and put us in the Saturday night championship game with the Ridgeway Owls, who had defeated Tri-County in the other semifinal game. We had won all three games against Ridgeway the year before, so we knew we could beat them, although they did have some very good outside shooters. With their offense, we knew we couldn't afford to let them get going from beyond the arc, as North Harrison had done against us the week before.

All day Saturday the game was never far from my mind. I arrived at the gym early Saturday evening, watching the other games that night. There were some interesting games, but I was thinking about our game, focused on what we needed to do. The minutes dragged by until finally it was time for us to go get dressed. In the locker room, we were a little nervous because we really wanted to win our

The 2003-04 Gilman City Hawks pose for a photo after winning the 2004 Gilman City Invitational Tournament. Front row from left: Sawyer DeWitt, Jacob Webb, Daniel Prindle, Daniel Dennert, and Kyle King. Back row from left: Coach Brent Burke, Jarett Webb, Heath Oram, Kaleb Wilson, Benjamin Herrold, Matt Houser, and Chad Cole.

tournament. We had come close to doing so the year before, losing in the title game, so now we wanted to finish the job. Another championship game loss in our tournament would be very frustrating. Adding to our anticipation was the big crowd on hand, but at least we were playing on our home court.

When the game started, all nervousness disappeared. We were too busy playing to think about what was on the line.

Ridgeway came out firing threes and took an early lead. Our offense started slowly, which led to a 15-8 Ridgeway lead at the end of the first quarter. The Ridgeway crowd was loudly cheering each three, but we weathered the storm, showing our resilience with a great second quarter. At the half, the championship game was a 22-22 tie.

After a low-scoring first half, both teams' offenses exploded. Both teams could see a tournament championship 16 minutes away, and both teams were furiously putting up points in an effort to outgun the other. We narrowly outscored the Owls, 19-18, in the third quarter to take a 41-40 lead into the final quarter. Our offense was rolling in the second half. Kaleb and Jacob were mixing in outside jumpers and drives to the basket. I was going to work in the post, making a high percentage of my shots and getting to the free throw line. Our team was avoiding the turnovers that occasionally slowed down our scoring and drew the ire of Coach Burke. Aaron Fitzpatrick was powering the Owls' offense, scoring nearly half of his team's points. Levi Price added 15 points for the Owls with his outside shooting.

The intensity of that game in the second half was about as high as any game I played in. With the tournament championship on the line, there was an almost Districts-like atmosphere. There was an exhilarating ebb and flow of momentum as we traded big shots and plays with Ridgeway. In the final quarter, our offense kept its torrid pace, again scoring 19 points during an eight-minute period.

We were able to slow down Ridgeway's offense in the fourth quarter, giving us a bigger lead. Late in the game, I quickly converted a fast break layup just as I got fouled and went flying into the padding on the wall behind the hoop. Our crowd cheered tumultuously and Ridgeway called a timeout. During our brief celebration as we headed to our bench I thought, we've got this now. We made a few free throws down the stretch and won 60-50. We were the Gilman City Invitational Tournament champions.

Kaleb and Jacob had scored 14 and 11 points, respectively, providing the speed and tempo for our offense. I finished with 21 points and 11 rebounds, a good game in a championship game. Many players hit a key shot or provided stellar defense. It was a team achievement, our highest so far that season. It was the first time any of the players in my class and below had won a tournament. We had won our tournament and made the community proud. The next issue of the weekly Bethany Republican-Clipper had a picture of me shooting over Fitzpatrick, giving our team two newspaper pictures in one week.

The three tournament wins improved our record to 10-6. We had won seven of our last eight games, including wins over some very good teams. Our offense and defense were kind of coming around at the same time. We were playing well as a team heading into February, the last month of the season before Districts week. The remainder of our season was full of possibility.

CHAPTER 8

In some ways unfulfilled potential can be worse than simple failure. When you know you are capable of doing something well and don't, it is very frustrating. Our team was like this at times during my junior season. We would win some big games to show what we were capable of, and then produce confounding, disappointing efforts. As our season went on its up-and-down journey, we developed a maddening inconsistency.

It was one of our lesser performances that was part of a change in the tone of our season. We had a week with games against North Daviess and Grundy R-V. Since the North Daviess boys team had ended their season when they could no longer maintain five eligible, willing players, we picked up a forfeit win. This left only the game at Grundy that week, the week before the HDC Tournament, which took place before the end of the regular season HDC games. A win at Grundy would keep our momentum from the Gilman Tournament going and keep our hope of winning the regular season HDC championship alive. It was also somewhat of a rivalry game after the epic battles the two schools had a few years before when my brother was in high school. Grundy R-V was having a rebuilding year, so we should have won the game.

It was similar to the North Harrison game in that we came out flat and our opponent started off hitting everything. Within minutes, we were facing a double-digit deficit. We sort of woke up from our early daze to rally late in the first. We cut the Grundy lead to four points by the end of the opening quarter. We couldn't draw any closer in the second quarter, playing only marginally better to trail by five at the half.

Besides everyone on our team deciding to have an off night in the same game, our problem was that Grundy's Brad Rains was on fire, hitting backbreaking three-pointers to crush our feeble rally attempts. Rains was too fast that night and he scored his 1,000th career point in the contest.

None of us stepped up to lead our sluggish offense. Jacob had 11 points, but it wasn't enough to offset our turnovers and low shooting percentage. I had 14 points, but I missed way too many shots from close range. I needed to be more efficient with my shots to help our team.

We trailed by eight heading into the fourth quarter. We cut the lead by a few points with some pressing, but we couldn't come up with the shots or plays to put us in front. We lost 56-49. After this loss and our forfeit win over North Daviess, our record was 11-7, 5-2 in HDC play.

It was a tougher-than-usual loss to deal with or explain. We had played much worse than we had most of the season. Later, Kaleb said we all played like we were high. Basically, we couldn't explain our poor play. Maybe it was a letdown game after the Gilman tournament, or maybe we were just a very up-and-down team. Whatever the reason, it was a surprisingly sloppy and uninspired effort on our part. Even though Grundy was in a rebuilding year, you just couldn't come into Galt and win without bringing your best game.

However, in the world of high school basketball, there is a lot more than on-court failures that can derail a season. Simply put, many high school kids drink alcohol, and an MIP would most likely end a player's season. All of us players had to sign a contract before every season saying we wouldn't use illegal drugs or alcohol during the season. To violate this is supposed to mean a dismissal from the team, according to the contract. The majority of the players who signed the document didn't give a thought to the fact they had no intention of doing what they signed to do. About 90% of high school boys at Gilman drank alcohol (or said they did) when I was in high school. This behavior is a known and seemingly accepted fact among the community, teachers, and students, so I don't know why the school mocks common sense with the contract. Probably to give them freedom to act should a player acquire an MIP.

Students always talked about their partying weekends on Monday. I don't drink or go to those types of parties, which made me somewhat of an outsider. The unsolicited stories let me catch up on the fascinating exploits of my fellow students. They were sometimes entertaining, and they broke up the drudgery of Mondays. They livened up the conversations at the lunch tables.

The Monday of the HDC Tournament, however, the weekend stories carried a darker tone. According to the rumors, two prominent players on our team had gotten MIP's while driving through Iowa.

The school was buzzing that day. Would the players be suspended or kicked off the team? Were the stories true? What would the school do to investigate? Word was surely around town. We had become a team overshadowed by scandal, which is no fun at all, unless you are Terrell Owens.

Coach Burke started practice Monday with a speech about how dangerous and foolish he felt underage drinking was, particularly when mixed with a heavy dose of stupidity. It was similar to an earlier pre-practice lecture during softball season when crazy behavior while under the influence had injured a player enough to miss some games. How did this happen? Think asking someone to punch you in the stomach to see if you could take it and having the puncher miss low.

After the opening speech, we played through a practice nearly devoid of the usual chatter. Many players were somewhat tense and unable to focus completely on the practice, with thoughts and worries circulating in the back of their minds.

The next day brought our first-round HDC Tournament game with Winston. We were seeded higher as the No. 3 seed, but Winston had defeated us by one point earlier in the year, when I missed the potential game-winner. The career series for players in my class against the Redbirds was 2-2 and almost every game against Winston was a physical, close contest.

The bus ride up to the site of the tournament, North Harrison High School at Eagleville, was quieter than usual, as the previous day's practice had been. We were a little concerned about the future makeup of our team, not knowing if a couple of our players would be kicked off the team. It was tough to focus on the game at hand up until the game actually started, which reestablished our world for a little while as four eight-minute quarters within the lines of the basketball court. Once the game started, we were too busy battling Winston to think very much about other things. For me, most non-basketball thoughts during games were brief and random, what Jerry Seinfeld called "shallow, fairly obvious observations."

Winston again used a 2-3 zone defense that had made things difficult for me in the post in our Gallatin Tournament game. They had three defenders near the basket, and one of them almost always seemed to find me when it was time to go for an offensive rebound. The traffic jam of defenders around the basket also made post scoring difficult.

On this night, I worked hard to get set up and get the ball in the post, as usual. My teammates used precise passing and lobs to help me get the ball where I could score some for our team. Kaleb was having a very good game. He hit a lot of shots along the baseline and out into the corner. When he got the ball in the corner,

Winston had to go out and guard him close or keep two defenders in the post. Depending on what Winston did, Kaleb or I could get a good scoring opportunity. In contrast to the last time we played Winston, I had a very good shooting night. Despite Winston's good defense, I started the night hitting every shot I took. It is a great feeling when you're on a roll shooting, seeing even your most haphazard shots splash through the net. I made 9 of the 11 shots I took from the field that night.

It was a close game for the entire game. Neither team could build any sort of a lead. There was tremendous effort and intensity by both teams in this HDC Tournament game. In the end, we held on to our paper-thin lead to win 54-50. Kaleb and I both had 18 points. We both had good nights on the same night, which coupled with a steady, low-turnover effort from the rest of the team to power us into the HDC Tournament semifinal game. We had shook off any distractions or controversy around our team and played well enough to win against a team that seemed to be almost exactly at our level. Our next opponent would be tournament host North Harrison, a No. 7 seed that had knocked off No. 2 seeded Ridgeway, again showing how dangerous they were, especially when they were playing on their home court. After the Shamrocks' Homecoming onslaught against us a few weeks ago, we were aware of this.

By the North Harrison game Thursday night, the MIP issue had mostly gone away. Nobody talked about it, and things went back to normal. We found out both players would keep right on playing. If they could still play, there didn't seem to be any reason for anyone to discuss what had happened. Our principal, Mr. Tolen, later said he called some courthouses in Iowa, trying to find out if anybody from Gilman City had been issued an MIP in those counties. In the end, it seemed that little was done to investigate the issue, at least at the public or semi-private levels. There was no "this is our investigation" told to the community by the school. With no apparent hard evidence, the issue went away with no action taken.

Mr. Vorthmann, our Social Studies teacher, was angry about the whole issue. He thought not enough had been done to get to the bottom of the issue. He said there was a double standard at Gilman City based on what family you were from and what you contributed to the basketball team. As one person with a limited view, I can't really say if this is true or not. I wasn't really interested in thinking about such things at the time.

I was just glad the distraction was over. I was ready to focus on playing basketball, not the misadventures of my teammates. Perhaps I should have cared more what happened, perhaps not. I really didn't care very much what they had or had not done or what they were dealing with. As far as I was concerned, the issue was over.

With the basketball team focus again on the court, we were ready to avenge our earlier loss at North Harrison. As mentioned earlier, the HDC Tournament is a huge social and cultural event for the area. Semifinal night is usually an intriguing night of drama. Four consecutive games are played (two boys and two girls semifinal games), providing several hours of the best basketball the HDC has to offer. Many fans stay for all the games this night, watching players synonymous with their schools and towns battle for coveted spots in the iconic HDC Tournament championship games.

Our game was the last one of the night. After the North Mercer boys defeated their rival Newtown-Harris and the Mercer and North Harrison girls won spots in the girls championship, it was our turn to take the stage.

North Harrison again came out firing, but we were ready for them this time. We took a double-digit lead in the opening quarter. When we got going, our offense was one of the HDC's best. We had multiple players who could score. We could score in a variety of ways, with our guards, forwards, or center. Our defense could also be formidable at times. This night we focused on stopping North Harrison sharpshooter Josh Smith. We were more prepared to defend him this time. We kept Smith mostly under control, holding him to 12 points, which helped us hold on to a narrow halftime lead.

We managed to play at a higher level in the second half, playing some of our best basketball of the season. In the third quarter, we began to increase our lead. It was my turn to lead the charge offensively in that period, attacking the Shamrocks from the post and even hitting an outside jump shot. I had another efficient shooting night, hitting seven of 10 shots and all seven of my free throws. Our offense was rolling in that second half.

Our lead slowly increased, and by quarter's end we had North Harrison on the ropes. Our offense continued its march to the championship game in the fourth quarter. It was now Jacob's turn to lead our offense. He took the game over in that final period, burying North Harrison with a barrage of three-point shots. Jacob had an incredible outside shooting streak that night. He made something like six or seven threes that night. It was one of those times when you knew his shots were going in as soon as he released them. Jacob led us that night with 26 points. I added 21.

The game became a rout with our second-half offensive brilliance. We won going away, 74-58. It was one of our best games of the year. Referee Alan Berry, who lives near Galt, was impressed with our performance. As he ran by our bench late in the game, he yelled, "How the hell did you guys lose to Galt?" It was an interesting question, one that spoke to the unpredictability of the HDC that year and to our inconsistency at times.

We had now won nine of our last 11 games played. Our record was 13-7, counting the forfeit win over North Daviess. The win put us in the HDC Tournament championship.

The next day in our ITV class we spent a fair amount of class time talking with the Eagleville girls about the tournament championship games, since both of our teams would be playing North Mercer for the titles.

We had an opportunity to make history that Saturday night in Eagleville. Gilman City hadn't won a boys HDC Tournament since the 1970s, when my dad and Heath's dad played. It was an opportunity for us to become one of the great Gilman teams people talk about.

I believe it was during that HDC Tournament in the 1970s that my dad was a part of a story still talked about around Gilman. Gilman was clinging to a small lead late in the game. The other team was trying to foul Dad since he wasn't a great free throw shooter. Dad ran all over the court to avoid being fouled, laughing as the opposing player tried in vain to catch him. Dad says he never left the court, but the stories have grown over the years, so now lots of people talk about him running into the bleachers to avoid being fouled. Dad says if you give them a few more years, they will have him out in the parking lot hurdling cars in his effort to avoid being fouled. In any event, Gilman won the game and a classic chapter of Gilman hoops history was added.

Now it was our turn. We would face strong competition for the conference tournament title in the North Mercer Cardinals. They had several experienced, fundamentally sound players. They had excellent three-point shooters and ran their offense with machine-like efficiency.

Saturday night brought our game, again the last game of the night. It was the tournament's biggest night, with both the third place and championship games for girls and boys. The big North Harrison gym was packed and a few radio stations were present to broadcast the games. The atmosphere was intense, electric. The GRC doesn't have a conference tournament, so it was a unique experience in the area.

Near the end of the girls' championship game, we went to our locker room to get ready. As we rose to file out of the bleachers, our old Ag teacher and the current Ag teacher at North Harrison, Mr. Craig, wished us luck. Most of the crowd seemed behind us as we went up against the top-seeded, powerhouse North Mercer Cardinals.

As Coach Burke talked strategy and drew plays on the chalkboard, there was some nervousness among us from playing in the big game. For me, all nerves went away as we ran out on the court, fired up and ready to take on anybody.

I have good memories of about every game we played, but a few of the big ones stand out. This HDC Tournament Championship game was one of the big ones. My memory of that night is almost surreal, yet strikingly vivid. I can see the big plays that night, the players involved, the big gym and all those people, and the gleaming trophies by the scorer's table. This was our moment, our opportunity, our destiny. We were ready to play.

We were not ready. In short, the game was a disaster. Our own personal Battle of Waterloo. Mercer crushed us from the very start of the game. It was another train-wreck start for us. Our feast-to-famine offense was most definitely in famine mode during the first half. In that desperate first half for our offense, I contributed a grand total of one point. We had a pathetic disgrace of a performance in a huge game.

Meanwhile, Mercer's Jeff Girdner was unstoppable. Mixing threes and forays to the basket while all the while moving, he was outscoring our whole team. It was one of the most dominating high school performances I have ever seen, and it came at our expense in the HDC Tournament Championship game.

By halftime it was pretty much over. But if nothing else we were not quitters and we knew how much better we could play. Coach Burke decided to try an adjustment that would benefit us down the road. We decided play a box-and-one defense against Mercer. In it, the "one" was a defender who would closely guard Girdner wherever he was. The "box" would be the other four defenders, with one roughly at each corner of the lane. I like the idea of running box-and-ones or triangle-and-twos in the HDC, where teams often feature one or two dominant players who do most of the scoring.

The box-and-one worked well for us. Mercer recognized it quickly, but it slowed Girdner down quite a bit from his torrid start. He wasn't stopped, but at least slowed down. Our offense came around a little in the second half, too. Like my teammates, I kept working on offense and converted a few field goals. We played a fairly competitive game in the second half. It was good we kept playing hard despite the huge disappointment of the first half.

With that big lead from the first half, Mercer won easily, 54-29. None of us had played very well. Jacob led us with 11 points. Kaleb added six. In my first HDC Tournament Championship game, I scored only five points, one of the lowest outputs of my career. Girdner finished with 36 points. After working so hard to get to the championship and dreaming of winning it all, our HDC championship game experience had been an incredible disappointment, a blowout loss. We felt like we had let down our fans, our town, and ourselves. We had wasted our opportunity.

After the game we received our second place trophy, a reminder of all we had accomplished that week, despite its unfortunate end. Second in the HDC Tournament is still something to be proud of, although I felt like the horse that got second in the 1973 Belmont Stakes by 31 lengths to Secretariat.

We got a second chance against Mercer quickly as our next game was a regular season home game with Mercer. We could use our bad loss as a learning experience and use home-court advantage to try and pull the upset. People at school were excited about the rematch with Mercer. Students made signs and decorations for the games. It was like a miniature Homecoming celebration. In art class, Desiree had the creative insight to make a sign reading "Play them Cards right," a word play on North Mercer's Cardinal mascot.

This time we were ready to play Mercer. It was obvious from the start that this game would be different than the annihilation in the HDC Tournament. The game started out close and stayed that way. We used the box-and-one defense to slow down Girdner, which slowed down Mercer's offense. They worked through their offense again and again, looking for openings, but our defense held its ground. We also ran our offense patiently, avoiding the bad shots and turnovers that had hurt us in the previous game with Mercer. It was tough for us to get a lot going on offense against Mercer's tough defense, but we kept working and looking for ways to attack the Cardinals. As we kept working, we got some open jump shots for our guards or good post scoring opportunities for Kaleb, Sawyer, or me. In a complete turnaround from my disastrous performance in the HDC Tournament Championship, I shot at a high percentage in the game. Kaleb had a good shooting night as well, and he hit several big shots for us as we battled with the HDC's best.

Mercer's coach, Dan Owens, was given a technical in the first half, reflecting the game's intensity. Coach Burke had Jacob shoot the free throws, but he was unable to make them.

Points were tough to come by as both teams provided great effort and stout defense. Our crowd gave us strong support, cheering us on in our bid for an upset and revenge. When we hit a big shot to take a brief lead late in the first half, the Gilman faithful erupted.

Mercer grabbed a narrow lead just before the half, but we kept working our offense and playing the box-and-one as we hung on into the second half. We kept Girdner under control, but his fellow senior Derek Holmes stepped up for Mercer and nailed jump shots whenever he found an opening in our defense. He led the Cardinals with 14 points. Mercer held its narrow advantage late into the fourth quarter. We had to foul at the end of the game and Mercer converted its free throws, striking down our upset bid. Mercer won 45-34, with the final margin of victory padded by the free throws.

We played a very good game, but we just didn't play well enough to beat Mercer. I scored 13 points and Kaleb had 12 points, but neither of us had come up with the big shots down the stretch to put us over the top against an experienced and well-coached Mercer team. I always remember how hard we had to work for every point and rebound in our showdowns with Mercer. Although we had come up just short in our effort to pull off an upset/get revenge/play them Cards right, our confidence had been built back up after it was crushed in the HDC Tournament debacle. We knew we could beat Mercer if we faced them in Districts.

The second straight loss to Mercer dropped us to 13-9 on the year. It was also our third loss in conference play on the season, ending any realistic chance we had of winning the HDC regular season title.

Our season so far had been a tour of the highs and lows a high school team can experience. Now, as we headed down the season's homestretch, our team appeared to be in decline. Our season was an example that often times there isn't any one thing that causes a good team to start losing, but a combination of events. For us there was a parade of setbacks and challenges that kept coming and coming, something we could resist at first but eventually they all overwhelmed us, leading to an unsightly losing streak late in the year that began with the two Mercer losses. There was the game we got ambushed and outgunned at North Harrison. They came the pathetic performance at Grundy R-V, where our incompetence was impossible to explain. Then came the MIP controversy with the questions and the heavy sociological and moral issues it brought up. The issue didn't lead to anything, but it weighed on the players involved. It was an unnecessary distraction that disrupted the focus so critical to success in athletics. Another challenge came in back-to-back games against the best team in the conference, North Mercer. That naturally led to back-to-back losses, which didn't help the confidence of our team. The psyche of a high school boy is usually more fragile than it appears on the surface.

These setbacks had come but we had only lost some games here and there. We hadn't fallen, but we were wavering. We were hanging on to our season, but our lapses in some games were ominous signs.

We would later be able to see the losses to Mercer as the start of our late-season derailment. Our next game was at home against Ridgeway. We had dominated Ridgeway over the first two years of my career, winning all four of our games with them, three times by double digits. But this night was different. We mixed shoddy defense and an alarming amount of turnovers to stretch our losing streak to three. To their credit, Ridgeway was improving rapidly and played very well that night. Unfortunately, we seemed to be heading in the opposite direction. We did have a few good moments, particularly on offense. Our guards did a good job getting fast breaks started for us, which limited Ridgeway's ability to press. I was able to contribute a lot in the post, scoring 16 points on seven of 11 shooting. We played a close game and could have won and maybe got ourselves back on track, but we were just a little too sloppy to get the job done. We played below the level we had been at for much of the season. We had played good defense and been efficient on offense in our loss to Mercer. Against Ridgeway, we seemed to be a team arrogantly trying to outscore our opponent. The trouble was that Ridgeway was rolling on offense while we were playing fairly mediocre on offense. Our offense was good enough to keep us in the game, tantalizingly close to victory, but we lost, 61-53. We had a losing streak on our hands.

Next was our final road and HDC game, at Winston. After that was a home game with Osborn, then Districts, so we needed to get back on track in a hurry.

Ending our three-game losing streak against Winston would not be easy. Winston was in the top half of the HDC, and the Redbirds always seemed to give us a hard-fought game. Earlier in the year, they had defeated us by one point in the Gallatin Invitational Tournament and we had picked up an exhausting 4-point win over the Redbirds in the HDC Tournament. My class' career record against Winston was 3-2. When the two of us played, it was always an effort-laden, riveting ballgame.

This game was more of the same. Both teams frantically scrambled for the lead, with neither team able to shake the other. With both teams playing aggressive defense, scoring was hard to come by. There didn't seem to be any easy buckets in this game. In all three games with Winston that year, both teams' final scores stayed in the 50s.

In addition to another solid all-around effort from point guard Cody Lang, Winston got a tremendous effort from forward Daniel Williams that night. Williams scored from the outside and the inside that night, making him difficult to guard or keep track of.

There was a lot of physical play in the post, with intense battles for rebounds and position in the post. On one play, a Winston player boxed me out aggressively for a free throw. This happened a lot, but he caught me just right this time and bruised my thigh pretty good. Our games with Winston were usually physical but clean, so bumps and bruises like this were common in the series.

Like all my teammates, I was playing with the hunger of a team desperate to win. I kept battling and working, with the Redbirds making me earn every point and rebound. I finished with nine points, 10 rebounds, and four blocks, a decent all-around performance. Jacob was attacking the Winston defense. He mixed threes with aggressive drives to the hoop to help us hang with the Redbirds.

In this close game, we strained against Winston along the great win-loss line of sports. A win on the road would be huge, a statement we were back on track and ready for Districts. Our three-game losing streak would be over, viewed as a minor hiccup of close losses against tough competition. A loss would be four in a row, a sign we were regressing. It would be a real problem, a weight of failure weighing us down and pulling us deeper into our slide.

We faltered late in the final quarter. Despite our great effort and the fact we really didn't play that bad, we lost 57-52. The losing streak stretched to four. It was one of those games that was close throughout, only one team (Winston) happened to hit a few more shots at the very end, when it was most critical. Instead of celebrating a hard-fought "we're back!" victory, we sat in our silent dressing room after the game, wondering what happened to our team in the last few weeks. Our most recent win, over North Harrison in the HDC Tournament, was a distant memory. That sharp contrast between winning and losing is one of sports' great selling points, but it's not really fun to be on the losing side.

Our season's steady decline continued. It was a slow, painful process we now seemed powerless to stop. We headed into our Senior Night season finale game with Osborn with one more chance to end the losing streak before Districts. It was also a chance for some payback for Osborn's apparent running up of the score on us a year before.

What the game with Osborn appeared to be was our team hitting rock bottom. Despite our home crowd and Osborn being a very beatable team that season, Osborn dominated the game. The Wildcats led throughout, snuffing out our weak rallies. When the game mercifully ended, Osborn won 72-57. It didn't really seem that close. Our derailment was complete. Our losing streak was now five games, with Districts looming ahead, waiting for the kill shot on our season. Teams try to peak for the season-ending District Tournament, but we had valleyed for Districts.

We had to refocus before Districts, to find whatever we had when we were winning nine of 11 games and go back to it. The District Tournament is a new opportunity, a second act of the season. It was the perfect opportunity for a team in desperate need of a fresh start.

CHAPTER 9

Ambivalence, or having strong feelings both for and against something. In this case: the District Tournament and its importance. The District Tournament is not fair. One game, one play, one moment overshadows hours of work and dozens of games. Regular season accomplishments, such as scoring 24 points in an anonymous mid-season Tuesday game, while not being forgotten, often get blurred or put in context of District results. Far weightier than outside commentary, however, are the memories of the player. District games often dominate my memories of basketball, sitting there in my mind, ponderous, unwieldy, and sharpened a little by time. In sports, a player's career is often defined by one moment, and the District Tournament often screams, "I am that moment. Beware!" It is not fun or fair to have a year or career of work and dedication summed up by one mistake at a critical point. Ask Bill Buckner or Ralph Branca about this.

District games are so important, their influence so disproportional, that they can be unnerving and even terrifying to play for some. High school is a massive collage of experiences, triumphs, and letdowns. With Districts being very important in basketball and basketball being very important in high school, a few pressure-packed hours can dim the importance of thousands of other hours of shaping experiences. Rarely is there such potential for euphoria or disappointment in other high school experiences. It is the win-lose contrast of sports at the highest level I have experienced.

The District Tournament is very fair. Its win-lose contrast is the great equalizer. In a world of everything in moderation and the truth being somewhere in between, there is a thrill, even comfort, in this definite, win-lose divide of sports. All schools start at Districts, with winners playing on. All you have to do to experience the glory of a District Championship and state playoffs is to win. Likewise, every team that loses is done. The District Tournament gives all teams and all players an equal chance at glory, a second chance for teams that played poorly during the regular season.

The District Tournament consists of the biggest games of the year, so players can become heroes with one game, one play, one moment. In this way, the District Tournament rewards players who are at their best when the team needs it most. This seems fair and reasonable, the flip side of an athlete forever remembered for one costly error. The District Tournament elevates players into heroes, giving them more attention than most will experience the rest of their lives. Very few people cheer or yell when you buy a house or land a job.

I love the tournament, and yet I am almost overwhelmed by it. I think these like-dislike feelings come natural to sports, with its great divisions of winners and losers. The difference between winning and losing high school basketball games may never be greater than during Districts.

The problem was we looked very much like losers heading into Districts. We were 13-12 on the season, but we had played very poorly in the last few weeks of the season, closing out our regular season with a disturbing five-game losing streak. The skid was peppered with progressively pathetic performances. First came two tough losses against the HDC's best team, then two losses against teams we had defeated earlier in the year, and finally a 15-point home loss to a mediocre team most people expected us to roll over.

The losing streak was probably caused by several things, like getting annihilated in the HDC Tournament Championship game, off-court MIP distractions, a lack of focus at the end of a long season, the ups and downs of teenage basketball players, and a slow, steady, frightening, gnawing acceptance of losing.

Fortunately, Districts provided us with the fresh start we needed. The tournament was seeded before most of our late-season tumble down the stairs, so we got the No. 2 seed. Mercer was the No. 1 seed. It was the exact scenario I had brought up in the Dinner Bell after Districts the year before. We played the No. 7 seed in the first round, the Cainsville Redmen. After beating Cainsville by 21 points earlier in the year, it looked like a good first-round opponent for us. We could build back our confidence, rediscover the joys of winning, and hopefully have a stress-free win to move us into the District semifinals. However, we had shown an ability to lose to any team, even ones having poor seasons. The lower-tier opponent heightened the need to win and look good doing so. A loss to Cainsville to end the season would be disastrous. We needed to win by a comfortable margin to get our confidence and passion back. Fear and insecurity are not well served in Districts.

Before our game with Cainsville, we were completely focused on winning that specific game, putting the season's achievements and letdowns out of our mind. After losing five in a row, all our confidence, all our momentum had to be created within our District games. The tournament was a separate world, one week to redeem our up-and-down season.

One thing about our team, despite our lapses into mediocrity, was that when we played our best game and played as a team, we were very tough to beat. We had a good variety of types of players and featured several scoring options. We could tighten the screws and play stout team defense. Our team had a lot of big-game experience at this point. We were a team that could get on a roll for a few games. In short, we were a team built for the high stakes, intense games that are tournament basketball. We were built for this tournament.

Prior to the tournament, Jacob was in the station uptown. Someone asked him how our team was going to do in the District Tournament. Jacob summed up the feeling of our team. "We're going down there to win it," he said.

The short bus ride over to Pattonsburg, the tournament host, was unusually quiet. There were a lot of strong emotions and anticipation for the game, so nobody really said much. When we finally stepped out onto the court under the dome at Pattonsburg, we were ready to win.

Like a light switch flipping on, our team awoke. The poor Cainsville Redmen were overmatched against our suddenly revitalized team. On defense our hungry, seeking hands swatted away passes and shots and clawed for rebounds. Our offense, mostly on hiatus since our terrible end to the conference tournament, was back. Our attack came from all angles, with three of us scoring in double digits. By the time the first quarter was over, we led, 27-6. One impressive quarter appeared to have reversed our slide. We played on to a 41-18 halftime lead, always maintaining control of the game. We continued to pull away with another good half. The final score was Gilman City 73, Cainsville 39. Cainsville wasn't a high quality opponent, but we had still played our best game in weeks and taken care of business. We were back.

Next was the semifinal game against Worth County, a team that had improved a lot down the stretch. The Tigers of Worth County had knocked off the Tigers of Newtown-Harris in their first-round game.

The game was played on Wednesday, the day after our win over Cainsville. It was the last game of the night, tipping off around 9 p.m. Stewart Johnson sat on the stage by one of the baselines, broadcasting the game for KAAN radio.

The semifinal game with Worth County presented a great opportunity for us. Ever since watching the classic District Championship games at North Harrison the year before, I really wanted to play in one. Like my teammates, I was enthralled by the possibility of playing in such an intense, important game. The District Championship game and its atmosphere fascinated me, and I wanted to experience playing on that stage. If we could beat Worth County in that late-night contest under the dome, a berth in the District Championship would be ours.

Most teams get better as the season goes on, but the important thing is how much a team improves. Worth County had improved tremendously since we beat them by 17 in the Gilman Tournament.

The Tigers, pulling out all the stops for Districts, played a triangle-and-two defense against us. This defense is like the box and one, but two defenders shadow two offensive players while the other three defenders play a "triangle" zone defense, with one player at the top of the key and two on the blocks. It is definitely an unusual look for a defense, and it allows a defense to focus on two players rather than just one. The drawback, of course, is that it is easier to find an opening against a "triangle" of three defenders than a "box" of four defenders. The other three offensive players basically get to play three on three against the triangle zone, which opens things up more.

Worth County put its two defenders on Kaleb and Jacob. This put pressure on the rest of us not only to step up the scoring but also to create scoring opportunities for Kaleb and Jacob.

I think the different defense and good execution of it by WoCo kept our offense off balance at the start of the game. Our offense was pretty bad in the first quarter. At the end of that quarter we trailed, 12-6. We started finding some openings in the Worth County defense in the second, but the Tigers kept us at arm's length. At the half, we were losing 26-20. We just couldn't catch up with the Tigers, who seemed capable of staying just out of our reach all night. With 16 minutes of game time left, our season was in peril.

Fortunately, in the second half our offense was fully in attack mode. Individually and as a team, we picked apart the triangle and two. Matt Houser had a 14-point game. I found openings in their post defense and had 16 points and 12 rebounds. Jacob scored 11 points despite always having a defender following him. With WoCo really focusing on him, he set the rest of us up with 9 assists. We scored 41 points in the second half, more that twice what we managed in the first half. We barreled into the lead and held on in the fourth quarter despite a full court press defense from Worth County. We won 61-53, putting us in the championship game against an opponent we knew well, the North Mercer Cardinals.

Mercer was definitely the favorite. They were the No. 1 seed and had won both times we met earlier in the year. While we were 15-12 coming into the game, Mercer boasted a 23-4 record coming into the matchup. In their semifinal game, Mercer had churned out a 44-31 win over Ridgeway. Ridgeway had some very good players, as we knew firsthand, but they had succumbed to Mercer's stifling defense. We watched the game before our game with Worth County, and it had been a cold-blooded, machine-like, almost inevitable victory for Mercer. When going to the bench at one point in the game, Aaron Fitzpatrick, one of the Owl's best players, slammed both his hands into the bench in frustration. We knew the frustration that playing Mercer could cause. The four players in my class were 0-5 against the Cardinals.

However, we knew we could beat the Cardinals. Our best game could hang with any team in the area. Our record could be attributed to playing a challenging early-season schedule and our inconsistency. All it would take for us to win would be for us to play our best game, which we did every now and then. If we could play our strong team defense and run our box and one correctly, we could win. We had nearly beaten Mercer earlier in the year at home. It was our turn. It was our time. The collective will of our team was set on beating Mercer.

Friday was game day. The complex problems of College Algebra and the brilliant cynicism and metaphors of William Golding's Lord of the Flies did a fair job of distracting me during the day. However, my thoughts kept going back to the game. Most of my teammates I talked with shared my mix of nerves and excitement. We talked with the North Harrison girls in ITV class about the upcoming games. Their team was playing Worth County in the girls championship game and their coach made them carry basketballs around school all day.

Some of the teachers had a surprise pep rally for us during lunch. Snooks Johnson, who worked in the school's daycare department, came into the cafeteria in Gilman City attire wearing a sash that read "Granny Victory." Mr. Vorthmann talked a little bit about how proud of us the teachers and community were. At the end of the pep rally, the teachers sprayed us with silly string. We were inundated with about as much of the stuff as was sprayed on Kramer in that Seinfeld episode. It was a fun little surprise. Community support and excitement are a fundamental part of District basketball.

Eventually that school day was completed. There was that awkward little gap of time between when school ended and our bus left for Pattonsburg. Mom always fed us kids something good before our games. She taught Family and Consumer Sciences for a while at Gilman City and then became a Nutrition Programs Associate for the University of Missouri Extension Office, so she always knew good things to eat before a game, like spaghetti or pancakes. There usually wasn't a whole lot of time between the end of school and the bus departure, so I usually just relaxed and thought about game strategy. Sometimes I read or watched TV. It was usually a calm-before-the-storm period. I always prayed before our games. I sometimes prayed during this open time or on the bus ride or by myself in a quiet corner of the locker room. I never prayed that we would win because I thought that was selfish and a misuse of the privilege of prayer. God is about infinitely more than which team wins a game. I prayed that nobody would get hurt badly, that people would travel safely to the games, and that we would have fun and just do our best. I also asked Him to help me not be nervous. I didn't usually get real nervous before games, but I always asked for His help in dealing with any nerves I had.

There was definitely a sense of anticipation on our bus ride to Pattonsburg. Our excitement built during an intense girls championship game between Worth County and North Harrison. Pattonsburg's dome, which had a fairly high capacity, was absolutely packed. Both sides of the gym had row after row of people sitting shoulder to shoulder. Fans of the four schools playing that night as well as fans of other schools looking for exciting hoops games made use of every foot of bleachers. The crowd seemed huge, even under the great domed roof that seemed to dwarf everything.

We went to the locker room and got ready, only to have to wait a little longer as the girls' game went into overtime. Eventually, Worth County defeated the Lady Shamrocks of North Harrison in a heartbreaker. After a year of effort and then two days of waiting, it was now our turn to play for a District Championship. All the pride, achievement, and prestige of a District Championship were right in front of us, one win away. We were so close, yet the game itself was a huge hill we had to climb first.

Between the girls and boys games, the crowd spilled onto the edges of the court as people went to the concession stand or restroom. The mass of humanity kept us hemmed in as we went through our warm-ups. Looking into the crowd, I could see the traditional

Gilman crowd at its finest: friends; relatives; teachers; the school cooks; Goldie and Mona Lou, those Gilman superfans who were school secretaries for decades; the parents of our team, perhaps remembering great games of their own; our student managers, who were wearing shirts they had painted and decorated themselves; younger students, perhaps dreaming of their future epic games; grandparents cheering proudly; and just about anyone else I ever saw around town. They all roared during player introductions…"And a 6-4 junior, number 50, Benjamin Herrold!" Our District Championship game was on.

For all the buildup and everything on the line, the tempo of the game was slow and deliberate at the start. We had already played North Mercer twice and studied them on film, so we knew each other very well. We were feeling each other out, trying to find new ways to attack each other's defense. Both teams were also playing the patient, ball-moving offenses and strong defenses that got us to this point. All this led to a low scoring first quarter. After that first quarter, Mercer claimed a 6-4 lead.

By comparison, the second quarter was a shootout. We were running the box and one on Mercer's Jeff Girdner, with Jacob usually being the one to guard Girdner wherever he went. Mercer had seen us run this defense against them before, so they had worked on freeing Girdner with a variety of screens. We called out the screens on defense, also yelling and talking about where Mercer players were going. Coach Burke always wanted us to talk on defense, and we really communicated a lot in this game, which helped us play great team defense. Despite the extra attention, Girdner kept moving relentlessly. If we allowed him to find even the smallest opening, he could and would make us pay.

Slowly and with great effort, Mercer added onto its lead early in the second quarter. Midway through that quarter, the Cardinals led 16-8. However, we were a resilient team that knew how to deal with adversity. Our offense had too many options to be dormant forever. Kaleb hit a layup to spark a rally for us. I kept working for position in the post, hitting some shots for us as we slowly reeled in Mercer. Sawyer, with his quick first step and ability to elevate, got some more precious points for our team. By the half, we had trimmed Mercer's lead back to two points, 19-17.

The game's intensity had been building as the game went on and remained close. By the second half, the game atmosphere was electric, with the crowd erupting with each hard-earned bucket. The game was becoming a classic, high school basketball at its finest.

In the second half, both teams turned up the defense to an even higher level. Points were a precious commodity, with each bucket being the result of teamwork and great effort. Six points in a game like this was like 16 points in a regular game. Both teams were giving exhausting, almost frantic efforts at both ends of the court.

In the third quarter, we played our best defense of the season. Mercer simply couldn't score. Their scoring drought to begin the second half extended to two minutes, then three, then four. It was difficult for us to score as well, but we managed to hit a shot here and there, finally grabbing our first lead of the night during the third quarter. Meanwhile, Mercer still couldn't score on our defense. Five minutes without a point for the Cardinals, then six minutes. Our lead grew at an agonizingly slow rate. Near the end of the third, we were up 27-19. A 10-0 run to begin the second half. The crowd was beside itself. Fans from other schools were cheering for us, the underdog trying to topple a dynasty that had won several District titles in a row and defeated us twice earlier in the year. Victory was in the air. We were playing with incredible intensity and focus. Mercer must never score. Seven minutes of shutout defense…

Mercer would not fade away. It was now their turn to get up off of the mat in this epic struggle. Tyler Hartley made two free throws for Mercer to cut our lead to 27-21. We had held Mercer scoreless for seven minutes and 35 seconds, nearly a full quarter. They were still struggling against our defense, but Girdner was there to give Mercer a spark. He was hurting after a hard, but not malicious, foul from Chad. Our defense was all over him. Still, he somehow found a narrow window and drilled a buzzer-beating three to end the third quarter. Mercer's 5-0 run in the last 25 seconds of the third quarter cut our lead to three, 27-24. Girdner's three-pointer awoke Mercer and took away some of the momentum we had spent a nearly perfect seven minutes and 35 seconds building. Still, we had a small lead with a mere eight minutes between us and a sectional playoff game at Chillicothe.

Neither team would collapse and go quietly into the night. For all the pressure and energy under the dome, both teams responded with some great basketball.

Looking back on that game makes me think of Theodore Roosevelt's "man in the arena" quote. Our team was the man in the arena. We were striving and working to know "the triumph of high achievement." We were "daring greatly," so we would never be with the people Roosevelt called "those cold and timid souls who knew neither victory nor defeat." On this night of dreams, effort, and enthusiasm, we would win or we would lose. Whatever happened, our struggle to achieve something great was worthwhile.

Back and forth we went. A Cardinal hit a shot, then a Hawk answered. Players for both teams made huge plays. With a Mercer player reaching around one side of me, I caught the ball, spun away from the defender, and laid in a crucial layup just before Girdner could get there to contest it. Mercer's Derek Holmes tied the game with five minutes to go and then gave Mercer the lead with two free throws. Kaleb and Sawyer slashed to the hoop, fearlessly attacking the Cardinal defense.

A problem for us, with the physical play, was foul trouble. I played carefully for a while with four fouls. Then, late in the game,

Holmes drove to the hoop with only me in the way. I tried to stand as straight as I could, but the ref called me for my fifth foul. Holmes flopped and got the call. I had given it my all and had stayed in until very late in the game, but I would have to watch the last few minutes. It was the only game of the 80 I played in high school that I fouled out. Interestingly, I didn't get to shoot any free throws in the game. I got a nice ovation from the crowd as I headed to the bench to cheer on my teammates.

The game went on and was tied with under a minute to play. One minute to decide the District Championship. With 50 seconds to go, Jacob hit a short jumper to power us into a 34-32 lead. Two Mercer free throws then tied the game with 30 seconds to go. Both teams had a chance to win the game at the end of regulation, but both defenses held. On to overtime.

I usually played when the games were close, so it was weird to have to just watch what happened. I was much more nervous watching than playing because there was nothing I could do and no outlet for my energy.

Overtime was more back and forth swings of momentum. Both teams could land jabs, but neither could get the knockout punch needed. With under a minute to play in overtime, we clung to a 41-40 lead. Mercer had the ball. We tightened up the belts for one last defensive stand. I yelled with the crowd as we stopped them and Jacob got the ball. He dribbled up the sideline. With 9.5 seconds to play, he collided with a Mercer player on the sideline. It was a close play. The refs ruled it a turnover as the ball went out of bounds, which gave the ball to Mercer. Coach Owens called a timeout to draw up a play for Mercer.

What happened next was another piece of evidence that life is really unfair. After the close play on the sideline, Coach Burke was angry with the refs. He was arguing with the referee. Then the ref gave Coach Burke a technical, negating all that effort and skill with an arbitrary call. Mercer got two free throws and the ball.

The air went out of our crowd. Up by one, 9.5 seconds to go, District Championship, and Coach Burke had been given a technical. We were in disbelief. If only we had been in a position where one technical foul couldn't sink our hopes. If Burke said something to deserve a technical, that's very unfortunate. If Burke didn't say anything to deserve a technical and got one anyway, that's also very unfortunate. Whoever was to blame, it was a crushing turn of events beyond the control of those actually playing the game.

According to Coach Owens, Girdner told him to have Holmes shoot the free throws. As calmly as a man tying his shoes before a leisurely walk, Holmes made both free throws to put Mercer up one. They go the ball after the technical, so they inbounded the ball to Homes. He was immediately fouled so we could get the ball back. He again made both free throws. He hit eight of his 10 free throws in the fourth quarter and overtime. Also, eight of Mercer's 10 overtime points came on free throws.

Down three, we tried a last second heave to force a second overtime. I don't remember who shot it, but the shot missed. Mercer won 44-41 in an overtime classic that will always be remembered for its unusual ending. Our season was over. The Trenton Republican-Times' headline about the game summed things up: "Technical Foul Sinks Gilman City."

We played a good game, but after standing on the cusp of a District Championship we had fallen just short. We played a balanced, unselfish game. Kaleb and Sawyer both scored 10 points and I added eight points. Mercer's seniors led its scoring. Girdner had 15 points and Holmes added 12 points, many of which came from the foul line.

After the game, the referees, who none of us had seen officiate a game before, ran off the court. My brother Seth memorably sprinted after them, voicing his displeasure. The Pattonsburg staff put a stop

Our team reacts after the stunning end to our overtime
District Championship game in 2004

to this, but Gilman fans still talk about the incident with a smile.

Our locker room was stunned silence. Coach Burke apologized for getting the technical and told us it had been a very good season. The technical had been brutal, but we also looked back ruefully on all the little things we could have maybe done different or better to win the game in regulation. With so much on the line, with it being such a close and intense contest, with the unusual ending, it was one of the most difficult losses any of us ever had.

There were a few unpleasant events after the game. Coach Burke was escorted to the bus because of angry Gilman fans. There was a critical article in the Princeton Post-Telegraph saying Coach Burke had lost his brain on the trip over to Pattonsburg.

However, as fun or memorable or high-stakes as the games may be, life always goes on with its steady pace. We finished the year with a 15-13 record. Overall, it had been a good season. We had won the Gilman Tournament and taken second in the HDC and District Tournaments. We finished with a winning record despite a five-game losing streak late in the year. Despite the painful ending to the season, there had been many thrilling moments and good memories, like the big win at Newtown-Harris, winning the Gilman Tournament, our atonement win over North Harrison in the conference tournament, our run in the District Tournament, and beating our rival Tri-County on Homecoming night. The year had seen high and low points for our team, but the memories and experiences acquired were worth all the challenges and struggles.

A few of our players earned all-conference recognition. I was named First Team HDC All-Conference. On the year, I averaged 14.0 points, 8.1 rebounds, and 1.6 blocks per game. I had become a more efficient scorer, making 58% of the shots I took.

Jacob and Kaleb made HDC All-Conference Honorable Mention. Jacob averaged 12.0 points and 4.7 assists per game. Kaleb also had a good all-around season, averaging 10.4 points, 4.3 rebounds, and 2.8 assists per game.

Although we lost Jacob, Matt, Daniel, and Chad to graduation, the four players in my class would be back as seniors. Besides Kaleb and I, Sawyer and Heath were also coming off good junior years. During our junior year, Sawyer averaged 7.1 points and 5.3 rebounds per game. Of all our returning players, Heath led us in three pointers made and three-point percentage. He was also our primary ball handler.

The four of us were now seniors. The success of our team in our final season depended mostly on us.

CHAPTER 10

To a person currently experiencing it, senior year of high school is something of an iconic year. It is neither the greatest year of a person's life nor a waste of time coda to an otherwise productive high school career. It is something in between these two extremes, seemingly just another year made different by the fact it is your last in high school. Senior year is, to be sure, different than all those years parading in front of it.

The tangible differences between senior year and other school years are seen early and often during the year. There is the avalanche of paperwork related to college applications and scholarships, for one example. This led me to make lists of my community involvement, high school activities, and work experience for the dozens of forms that demanded the same information.

Then there are the changing views, priorities, and scheduling strategies teachers refer to as "senioritis." Sometimes senioritis just refers to the perceived laziness of senior students. When students get within a year of being out of school, they often don't see school as being that important. There is a desire to be somewhere besides Gilman City doing something besides going to school, which most students have been doing for almost all of their lives. This feeling can lead to both productive preparation and laziness. The preparation comes from those students who are a little tired of high school and ready to take life's next step, such as college. These students are eager for "real life" to begin and tend to focus more on college preparation and future goals than their high school duties. They are mentally boxed up and ready to move, which often hinders their commitment to high school activities.

On the laziness side are students who feel they are good people who have generally done enough to graduate and are ready to slide by for one more year, pick up a diploma, and be done with it all. They usually don't want to do any more than they have to. This can lead to cupcake class scheduling. Many senior schedules are peppered with Ag classes, P.E. classes, choir, yearbook, and "applied" something classes. Some seniors spend an hour as a teacher's aide. To be fair, these classes aren't always easy. What they are is a different way to learn. I had a great Ag Landscaping class during my senior year. I learned by actually landscaping a house, not just sitting at a desk, which is necessary in a lot of classes. I think it's good to have different ways to learn.

A lot of students who experience senioritis feel both effects— looking ahead with longing and occasional bouts with laziness. For example, I didn't need to take a class sixth hour of my senior year, so I was a teacher's aide. I did run some errands for teachers and office staff and I also used the hour to do homework and fill our college paperwork. This was productive preparation for future endeavors. Some days, however, I went to the gym and played pool with other senior teacher's aides. Other days I earnestly studied and poured over my NCAA Tournament bracket. On days like these I was a senior just enjoying my victory-lap year. Aside from being a teacher's aide, I did have some challenging classes, like Dual Credit English and Social Studies classes and a Physics class.

The yearbook for our class' junior year said we had "early onset senioritis." Some in our class did show an affinity for sleeping in class, skipping school, and procrastinating, other indicators of senioritis.

My class had eight students, and it was a fun class. There was always a lot of joking and one of us usually had a fascinating story to tell, such as the infamous "van night," stories about our families, or the Royals 2004 Opening Day game my friends and I went to. The Royals scored six runs in the ninth to win it, capped by Carlos Beltran's walk-off home run. We were a fairly close-knit class, barring just a few incidents here or there.

By senior year, a person's identity and character were mostly well-known among our class. Being with each other for so many hours and days and years led to us knowing a lot about each other. We knew everyone's middle name and birthday. There was definitely a familiarity to life at GHS, even for people not in the same class. We all knew most of the teachers well and all the things going on around the school.

However, as the old saying goes, familiarity breeds contempt. Gilman High had its share of feuds and bickering. Some things were the result of time-honored high school sources of discord, such as Prom and Homecoming decorations and themes. Then there were little daily disagreements and arguments about class fundraisers and other activities. There were people who just didn't like one another, thought someone was fake, or thought someone spread too much gossip. There were feuds and judgments about who was sleeping with whom. There actually seemed to be a lot of clashes between people during my senior year. Children and teenagers can be amazingly cruel to one another. I took a yearbook class that year and the yearbook staff decided on "Skiz-matik" for the title of the yearbook, a nod to the divisions in our high school.

I never really had cause to take part in these arguments. I am laid back and quiet by nature, so I never really took sides or talked about whatever controversy was going on. I didn't ever really open up to anyone else in high school. Maybe I had nothing to open up about. When I did talk to others it was usually about sports or incidental stuff. I listened to what others said, but I didn't care as much as I should have back then about what others were dealing with. I mostly just watched Gilman high school society with limited interest rather than playing a big role in it. If I said anything when there was a controversy or an argument, I usually just made a joke about it instead of a contribution to help resolve it.

Long before senior year rolled around, I was known as a guy who got good grades, loved sports, and did all right playing sports. I was All-Conference in basketball as well as Academic Team. I was quiet, but occasionally funny. I didn't drink or party. In my class, this didn't make me any better or worse than others, just different. It's like the sign in Bill's Barber Shop uptown that read, "Always remember that you are unique—just like everybody else." We all have something that makes us different.

I still got along great with my classmates and fit in just fine at school. I had my place. Still, despite having my place in Gilman High society, despite fitting-in in our small-school community, I was different and distanced at times.

This point was really made to me at Barnwarming during my sophomore year. I wore contacts for the first time. None of my classmates noticed because they mostly all came in various stages of drunkenness. Getting hammered was a perfectly normal thing for a GHS student to do on a weekend. I knew right then that I would never be a perfectly normal GHS student. I didn't want to conform to the pattern of this world.

In a paper for school dated March 5, 2004, the date of that awful District title game loss to Mercer, I wrote about William Golding's Lord of the Flies. I quoted a line from the book, when Simon talked to the Lord of the Flies: "the half-shut eyes were dim with the infinite cynicism of adult life. They assured Simon that everything was bad business." On a similar note, Golding wrote about "mankind's essential illness," how people can be so mean and selfish and flawed.

As high school went on, I could see many examples of "bad business" and "mankind's essential illness." I saw it in others as well as myself. The more I was let down by others and life's disappointments, the more I withdrew and focused on my own individual goals. I focused on things like writing, preparing for college, and basketball. I spent hours shooting at a hoop, working for something to be proud of, something worthwhile.

It was a couple years later, between my freshman and sophomore years of college, that God used a mission trip to New Mexico and a powerful sermon at my church to show me what was truly important, lasting, and worthwhile. My relationship with Christ, loving God, and loving others were the most important priorities for me.

Despite my differences, I got along well with my classmates. Many of my high school memories are of good and fun times. I stayed connected with my classmates and was forever linked to them by class activities, sports, and FFA activities. I'm still friends with people from my class.

One of these class activities came early in our senior year. It was Labor Day weekend when we parked cars at the Bethany Fair. This consisted of pointing cars to certain lots and directing them to where they were supposed to park. It wasn't real difficult to do, and we got paid $1,500 for the holiday weekend of work. We paid the freshman class a little to help out. There were some long days and at times the parking lots seemed to be at or near capacity, but it was fun. There were always things going on, lots of angry people demanding closer parking spots, and people we knew driving by trying to make wise cracks. It was also kind of fun being the only thing standing in the way of mass parking chaos, or so it seemed.

We all got to wear bright orange "Northwest Missouri State Fair" shirts and take turns riding around on 4-wheelers and golf carts. There were a lot of great stories from that weekend, like the racing of golf carts on the fair race track; Trace Adkins coming to town for a concert and getting mad when one of us parking extraordinaires directed a tour bus to drive over his electrical cords; people driving our sponsor, Coach Burke, crazy by constantly hitting the alarm button on our radios; or the final evening when, with all sanity long used up, some of the guys in our class turned the golf cart into a fire truck, complete with siren noises and a cup on the roof for a light.

We had a softball practice at 7 a.m. Labor Day morning before our final day of parking cars. Sawyer ended up getting a few brief hours of sleep the night before the early practice by sleeping on the field near home plate. This was an appropriate location since he was, after all, our starting catcher.

Senior year was a tapestry of contradictions and ambivalence. It was full of good and bad things, a microcosm of life. It was a year of preparation and laziness, of being alone and being connected, of divisions and being drawn together, of fun and drudgery, and of memories and dreams. It was one final lap at old GHS before being resigned to a class composite photo on the wall. It was also one more year for glory and achievement on the basketball court.

CHAPTER 11

It was still mostly dark outside as I stepped out on the morning of November 1, 2004. It seemed too early for me to function properly, but I was on my way into Gilman City for the first day of basketball practice. When you're 17, the only thing worse than getting up really early is getting up really early to run to the point of exhaustion. With only one gym to practice in and the junior high teams still in the last week or two of their season, our first practice was at 6:00 a.m.

My family lived about five or six miles out of town. Our house sat on a ridge on one of our farms, so when it was daylight a person in our yard could see the tops of the Gilman City water tower and grain elevator on the horizon, framing the town like uprights on a goalpost. On this morning that horizon to the east was just a faint glow in anticipation of the sunrise.

I started my Dodge Dakota pickup and headed for Gilman. As I drove along the dark, winding gravel roads into town, I thought about the season our team was about to start. It would be the last season for us seniors, one more chance to have success playing basketball, and hopefully to have a little fun. I have noticed how senior year in sports can be stressful. Whether it is a senior's desire to be out of high school or a fear of failing in the last chance at high school hoops, sometimes basketball for seniors can be very businesslike, almost an obligation. There is an intense desire to play well in the final year and a feeling that everyone expects big things in your final year. There are no excuses. Now or never. The pressure to do well in your last conference tournament, last home game, last Homecoming game, and last chance to win Districts can take some focus off having fun while playing. There is definitely a different feeling as a senior player. I think it is a healthy pressure; people push themselves and mature with a little pressure.

Of course, playing a game like basketball still retains some fun, even when there is pressure. The four of us seniors were mostly laid back and had a good sense of humor, so we usually kept that balance of having fun and striving to be our best and to win. Still, there were times when one could see pressure and expectations removing fun, when a player might hesitate against what was perceived as an obligation. After the season, one player admitted he really didn't have much fun playing. A teacher said he had noticed this while watching the player play. Another player said basketball was fun, but he didn't like how everyone was "so (darn) serious" about it. There were rightfully higher expectations of senior players. How they reacted to them often set the tone for the team.

I arrived at the school. A few other pickups were pulling into the gravel parking lot. Although it was empty, we parked in the back half of the lot, as the front part was reserved for faculty and staff. Some teachers could get pretty upset if students took the good spots and they had to walk extra, so we didn't try to start a first-come, first-serve policy on parking. Besides, what did it matter to walk an extra 30 yards when we were going to run so much?

A few smashed pumpkins lay on some streets, a reminder the night before had been Halloween. On Halloween, after the little kids had collected their quota of candy, some high school and even junior high students go around town throwing eggs, smashing pumpkins, and messing with things around town. They hope to find a cop or someone around town to chase them for some excitement. A few closet pyromaniacs even set things on fire, preferably in the streets. My rioting of choice is tearing down goalposts, so I never did any of this, but my fellow students assured me it was riotous fun. (With emphasis on the "riot.")

It was partially due to this Halloween tradition of being out late spiking pumpkins that led to groans of protest when Coach Burke announced our first practice was at 6:00 a.m. the morning after Halloween. Burke didn't want to hear any of it. "You better be there," he had warned us players.

One by one, the players started showing up. Our only freshman, Blake Johnson, was there. Our big group of sophomores, Steven Braden, Kyle King, Matt Eason, Jonathan Elder, Daniel Miles, and Zach Harris, all showed up. Our juniors, Jarett Webb and Daniel Dennert, arrived as well. I was there, Heath was there, and Sawyer was there. All we were missing were Kaleb and Coach Burke.

We dressed for practice and started shooting to warm up. Soon it was just a few minutes until six. No Burke or Kaleb. We started to talk, wondering where they were. Six o'clock came and went. We thought about leaving since Coach Burke wasn't there. It was a quarter after six. Where was he? We decided since we had all woke up and came in, we would scrimmage a little. We played full court, knowing we needed to work on our conditioning. Playing together helped us get to know our new players and regain a feel for game-style basketball.

After a little while, our school cooks arrived to begin preparing breakfast for those kids who ate the meal at the school. One of them came down to the gym to check on us, surely expecting to see us slogging through running and drills. Instead she saw a coachless group of players running and gunning up and down the court.

She went back to the school kitchen and called Coach Burke. Kaleb arrived soon after all this, just before Coach Burke showed up.

I think Burke saw him, but he couldn't really do anything since he had been late himself. Both Kaleb and Burke had had trouble with their alarms, either in setting them or falling back asleep after they went off. Burke talked with us for a while by the stage and then let us leave. It was a strange start, but now our season was off and running. The next day brought the start of normal practices.

We did have some strange and memorable practice incidents that year. Once, when Kaleb was guarding me in a scrimmage, my arm hit his nose, breaking it. He had broken his nose when he was younger as well. I'm not sure who caused the contact or how it happened, but he headed for the bathroom. We followed the trail of blood drops and found him calmly washing the blood off himself. Fortunately, he didn't miss any games due to the injury.

Another practice sideshow came just after we broke our final huddle one day. Sawyer took off a sock after a particularly exhausting practice. Standing in the lane on the court, he twisted the sock, wringing it out and producing a stomach-turning cascade of sweat.

Each practice brought us closer to our opening game. Our first game was at home, against Princeton on the Tuesday before Thanksgiving. Before our first game, we had the very important discussion about what music we would play when we came running out to warm up before the game. We chose "Thunderstruck."

Princeton had some athletic players, such as Jeff Lutzen and Jarin Gamet. Coach Burke boldly had us play man-to-man defense. We were fairly athletic as well, and we stayed in the man-to-man all game. Burke had me guard Gamet, who was listed at 6'3" yet did a lot of ball handling for the Tigers. I spent a lot of time guarding him on the perimeter. I almost always guarded the post, so this was different. Gamet was good at driving to the hoop so I focused on using good footwork while playing off him a little. From watching him play it seemed he did the most damage on drives to the hoop because of his long stride. I gave him a little room for the long-range shot and hoped he wouldn't hit too many. If he did start connecting from long range, I would have to guard him closer on the perimeter. This strategy of preventing many drives to the hoop worked reasonably well, and Gamet only scored seven points in the game. Overall, we played good man-to-man defense. We helped each other out and communicated, which makes it much easier to guard your guy.

Princeton played good defense on us, too. At the half, Princeton led 25-24. We came out after the break and played well. We outscored the Tigers 14-8 in the third to take a 38-33 lead into the final quarter. As had been expected, the seniors carried most of our scoring load. On this night, all our points came from the four seniors. I started the year with an 18-point, 11 rebound effort. Sawyer and Kaleb both scored 11 points, and Heath added six points while directing our offense as the point guard.

The way we were playing, we appeared poised to put the game away in the last quarter. However, Princeton battled back, led by the scoring of Lutzen. In the fourth, as our lead slowly melted away, our shots weren't falling. We scored only eight points in the final quarter. Our defense had some breakdowns late in the game, giving Princeton players lanes through which they could attack the hoop. Princeton pulled ahead with a few minutes to go. Unlike us, the Tigers held on to their fourth quarter lead. Princeton won 49-46, spoiling our home opener.

We had played well for three quarters, took a lead into the fourth at home, yet still lost when our shots wouldn't fall late.

Even though we were 0-1, we had shown we could effectively play man-to-man defense. In the Gallatin Invitational Tournament, we could use a mix of zone and man defenses. Our variety of players who could score for our team also added to our versatility.

Our first "last" of the season came in our last Gallatin Invitational Tournament. I was a little annoyed we hadn't done anything in the GIT during my first two seasons. Both years we had lost badly in the first round of the tournament and failed to win enough games to even win the consolation trophy. I wanted us to make an impact on the GIT, to make little Gilman High more than just an also-ran in the tournament. Despite our four experienced seniors, our team got the No. 5 seed. We would play the No. 4 seed, the Winston Redbirds, in the first round. We were both HDC schools, so an HDC school was guaranteed a spot in the winner's bracket. It would also be the third year in a row Gilman City and Winston met in the GIT. We had split the two previous meetings. The Gilman-Winston series had been very competitive in the preceding years. Our senior class was 3-3 against Winston. We had alternated wins in those six games, and it was our turn to win.

Sawyer forgot his warm-up pants, so we all went out without our warm-ups to look the same. We ended up not wearing warm-ups for the rest of the year.

We started slowly and the Redbirds grabbed an early lead. Cody Lang, Jared Lee, and Daniel Williams were all scoring a lot for the Redbirds. Winston led 20-9 after the opening quarter.

Our offense got going in the second, but Winston kept scoring in bunches to keep us at bay. Our offense got a boost from sophomore Kyle King, who had 12 points in the game. At the half, Winston was still up by 11, 36-25.

Finally, in the third quarter, our defense slowed down Winston's scoring. It was another physical, intense contest with Winston, but we slowly trimmed their lead. There was a lot of physical play in the second half, as five players fouled out in the game, but we took a slim two-point lead into the final quarter.

I gave us a good post presence in the game, scoring 20 points. Kaleb provided a lot of offense as well, scoring 14 points. After a slow first quarter, our offense was efficient against Winston. We did a good job working through our offense and finding open players and high-percentage shots.

The game stayed close in the final quarter. Neither team could pull away. Both teams were very familiar with one another after all our intense struggles. Now, here we were once again, battling for a spot in the GIT semifinals. We were going all out, and it was a fun game to be playing in.

The game was tied at 59 going into the final minute of regulation. Both teams missed a big free throw that would have given them a lead. With neither team able to score, we went on to overtime, deadlocked at 59.

We grabbed a narrow lead early in the four-minute overtime period. The physical play was catching up to us, as some of our key players began to foul out. We hit our free throws, though, and our lead grew to 69-63. I went to inbound the ball against Winton's press with just a few seconds left, realized I was the only senior left in the game, and inbounded the ball to Kyle, who held on to it and we won, 69-63.

This moved Gilman City to the winner's bracket for the first time since my brother's senior year. Our semifinal opponent was the Hamilton Hornets. Hamilton was a big GRC school, the No. 1 seen in the tourney. We were a tiny school, the No. 5 seed, a little fish looking for a big upset. The school size differential didn't mean much to me. We still, of course, played five-on-five. The advantage bigger schools have is a larger pool from which to draw talent and depth. At the high school level, depth is mostly an issue when you have foul trouble. I didn't see a potential lack of depth hurting us from a fatigue perspective. We played four eight-minute quarters, with breaks between quarters and for halftime and timeouts. We were in good shape after a month of conditioning and practice, so substitutions were more for strategy than rest. Also, the adrenaline of big games carries a player on. I usually didn't feel tired until after games, when the thrill of competition and playing were no longer giving me energy.

This year, we had a solid, experienced starting lineup and some shooting and defensive specialists off the bench. We could hang with about any high school opponent. This was a chance for us to make a huge impact on the tournament bracket, to take out the team the coaches had selected as the tournament's best in the seeding meeting. This could be a statement game, a statement for the HDC, Gilman City, and the season's potential.

Just before our game, we watched the other boys semifinal, Gallatin against South Harrison (Bethany). It was a close contest that went down to the final seconds. Gallatin pulled out the win, clinching their spot in the championship game. Now our team would battle Hamilton for the other spot in the title game.

Early in the game, we committed too many turnovers to make any kind of a statement. We played well enough to hang around, but we weren't being smart enough with the basketball early on. Part of this was good defense by Hamilton, part was our poor decision making. I wasn't getting good enough post position and I wasn't making good decisions as to what to do with the basketball when double teams came. After one quarter, Hamilton led 15-11. We cut down on a lot of our turnovers in the second quarter and ratcheted up our defense. We pretty much battled to a draw in the second. At the half, Hamilton led 25-20. We could beat this team, but we needed a rally.

Often in basketball, rallies come in a few frenetic minutes, a quick surge that comes like a lightning strike. Other times, as was the case for our team in this game, the momentum shift comes from a slow, steady buildup that eventually topples the opposition, like a wave that slowly builds and then crashes down. As the second half progressed, we played better and better. We slowly cut the Hornets' lead. We quit making turnovers and poor decisions. Heath's steady ball handling helped us do this. I got good post position, getting set up deep and digging in to hold by low-block position. When I got the ball, I could score some points for us or find an open teammate so they could get a good look. By working the ball like this we got good shots and spread around the scoring load. Kaleb had 15 points, Sawyer had 14, and I added 12. In that great second half, we showed how good we could be when we played disciplined, team basketball. We also gained control of the glass in the second half, securing rebounds with our collective box-out efforts.

By the end of the third, we only trailed by two, 37-35. We were in position to pull the upset. We had the momentum. As Coach Burke would say of the game: "We found a rhythm late in the game."

The fourth quarter was a classic struggle, full of big shots and all-out hustle plays. I remember diving for a loose ball just as a Hamilton player did the same from the other side of the ball. Naturally, our heads smashed together and a jump ball was called. I remember sort of a flash of light on the collision and then being helped up by my teammates.

Our defense was very good down the stretch, holding Hamilton to nine fourth-quarter points. We focused on stopping Shawn Englert and Sully Fairchild, who led the Hornets in scoring in the game.

We seemed to be very evenly-matched teams. We tied the game and it remained a tense, close contest for the rest of the game. With neither team able to pull ahead, the game went to overtime tied at 46. It seemed natural and almost inevitable that it would take overtime to decide this struggle in which neither team could gain much of an advantage. It was our second straight overtime game to start the tournament.

Overtime was more of the same. With less than 30 seconds to play, we had the ball with the game tied at 52. We worked the ball, looking for a good shot. With the final seconds slipping away, Jarett Webb, the junior who started alongside our four seniors, got open around the left elbow. We swung a pass over to him. He put up what was about a 17-foot jumper. I rolled over to the right block, working for rebound position. I looked up and watched Jarett's shot go in. We were up 54-52 with less than 10 seconds to go. The Gilman faithful roared, rocking the Gallatin gym. Hamilton got the ball to around half court and called a timeout with a couple of seconds to go.

Coach Burke had me guard the ball on the inbounds play from half court. The rest of our players matched up on the Hamilton players. Hamilton got the ball in and launched a desperation toss at the buzzer that didn't come close. We had won in an overtime classic, 54-52. The Gilman fans were going crazy and our team was going crazy on the court. We had knocked off the tournament's No. 1 seed. I yelled, "How about those Gilman Hawks!" However, my voice was lost in the din of the crowd. We went through the "good game" line, congratulating the Hornets on their great effort. Then we went to our locker room, enjoying the thrill of victory while beginning to turn our focus toward beating Gallatin in the championship game Saturday night.

Gallatin was the No. 2 seed and the tournament host. They had some good tall players as well as dangerous perimeter shooters. It would be a good test for us with the GIT championship on the line. There's a sense of pride in winning a tournament that you host, as we learned in winning the Gilman tournament the year before, so we knew Gallatin would be fired up and ready to play.

After practicing on Friday, Saturday was game day. We gathered at the school to load on the bus to go to Gallatin. To our dismay, the scenery of Gilman City had been dramatically altered. The biggest grain bin at the grain elevator had collapsed. There was only a heap of grain and metal where the huge bin had stood. In the days that followed local farmers loaned their trucks and semis to help haul the grain on the ground to Hoffman and Reed's Trenton elevator. It was an example of the community helping out in a time of need. Soon enough a new bin was built, but the collapsing of the old bin was startling for Gilman City residents.

We loaded on the bus and rode to Gallatin, thinking about the task at hand. We arrived and found the gym full of people. Extra seats had been put up on the walking area above the bleachers on one side of the gym. It was perhaps the biggest crowd we had ever played in front of, with the possible exceptions of the HDC Tournament and District Championship games at North Harrison and Pattonsburg. As we watched the girls' championship game between South Harrison and Trenton, our nervousness grew. It seemed as though everyone I had ever met or saw was there. Friends, family, acquaintances, people we had played against, people from multiple area communities, people from newspapers and radio stations, everyone. I was bad at talking in front of people, so how could I play basketball in front of so many? My success or failures that night would come before the eyes of my world. Eventually the time came for us to get dressed, so we went to our locker room, nervous and quiet.

After pre-game instructions, we walked down the stairs from our dressing room to the edge of our court, waiting for the janitors to sweep the floor. The Gallatin team came out of their room and stood next to us, waiting as well. Neither team spoke to one another. We didn't know them that well, and we all had on the mask of focus. The music over the speakers in the gym boomed that we needed to be ready.

We ran onto the court, the Gilman fans cheered, and any nervousness I had went away. We hadn't played in a GIT title game before, but we had been in some big games. We had played in the pressure cooker of the HDC Tournament Championship. We had stood toe-to-toe with North Mercer in a District Championship overtime thriller. This was our fifth appearance in a tournament championship game. We had just defeated Hamilton in our second straight

I block a shot during the GIT Championship game.

overtime game. We were ready. I may not have been good at talking in front of all those eyes, but this wasn't a speech, this was basketball. Playing basketball is natural for me. By this point in our careers, we seniors had experienced the big games. We would not be intimidated or back down. It didn't matter who was there or watching once we got on the court and could play.

We were fired up by game time. I was ready to attack Gallatin's defense, to go to work against Marcus Lacy and Andrew Adkison, their post players. We came out with a furious attack that kept the Bulldogs on their heels. They definitely knew right away they had a game on their hands, which they surely expected. I was attacking in the post, going right at whoever was guarding me, usually Lacy. I was able to get good post position and my teammates did a great job getting the ball to me. I had nine points in the first half, helping lead our offense. We used our aggressive zone defense to take a 13-10 lead after one quarter.

Gallatin was resilient as well, coming back with a very good second quarter. Kyle Hefley, who scored 12 points that night, hit two big threes in the second quarter to give Gallatin a narrow halftime lead. Our defense made up for the offensive struggles we had in that quarter. We got some good blocks and rebounds. In my efforts to shut down Lacy and Adkison, I had five blocks in the game. A yearbook photographer captured one of these, so as a member of the yearbook staff I felt obligated to put the photo in the yearbook.

At the half, Coach Burke urged us to keep up the intensity and reminded us we absolutely had to contain Hefley if we were to win.

In the third quarter, Gallatin tried to put us away, but we hung on. The Bulldog lead was as large as 11 and as small as four during the third. The third quarter ended with Gallatin up 33-29.

After I helped lead our offense in the first half, Kaleb scored a bunch for us in the second half. He used a mix of 3-pointers, free throws, and drives to the hoop to score for us. This was big because the fourth quarter was a high-scoring one.

Kaleb and Sawyer hit some free throws to cut the Gallatin lead to 40-39 in the middle of the fourth. We were on the brink of winning the tournament. Both teams were running and gunning in a wild final quarter. I hit an 18-foot baseline jumper. Adkison would counter with a big shot, as eight of his 23 points came in the fourth.

Kaleb hit a huge three for us with 2:17 to go that cut Gallatin's lead to 46-44. I thought this might propel us on one final rally for the win. Instead we fell into an offensive drought, falling behind 52-44 with 23 seconds to play. It was at that time that Kaleb was fouled shooting a three and made all three free throws. This briefly gave us life, making it 52-47. Unfortunately, Gallatin made their free throws late to close out the exciting game with a 56-47 win. Despite our offensive struggles in the final minutes, we played with all we had until the final buzzer. Dreams die hard.

We had played so well and played ourselves to the brink of winning the tournament, only to stumble in the final minutes. This was a frustratingly familiar feeling, as the four players in my class—Kaleb, Sawyer, Heath, and I—were now 1-4 in tournament championship games.

We had held Lacy to seven points, but we were hurt by Adkison's 23 and the big threes by Hefley that put Gallatin in the lead and put us into catch-up mode. Kaleb had a great game, with 23 points, five rebounds, and three steals. I added 13 points, seven rebounds, and five blocks. All of us had given tremendous effort. It was encouraging how well we had played in the tournament and how we had nearly beat Gallatin. In a local paper, Coach Burke said, "After this, we feel that we can compete with anyone."

After the game, we received our second place trophy. Second place in the GIT wasn't too bad, even though it burned that we hadn't won the thing. Both teams stayed on the court for the announcement of the GIT All-Tournament teams. Sawyer, Kaleb, and I were named to the team. My name was called just before the tournament MVP, so people said if we had won the championship game I would have been tournament MVP. The MVP award went to Gallatin's Kyle Hefley. It was nice to see three Gilman players on the All-Tournament team. The GIT was proof when we played disciplined and as a team, we could beat anyone. It was encouraging, despite the tough loss in the championship game.

We were now 2-2 on the season. Burke was right that our success in the GIT had built up our confidence. Gallatin and Hamilton were two of the toughest teams on our schedule, and we had played a close game with both, winning one. Our senior season could be a special one.

Our record of 2-2 was a good start with the teams we had played, but the schedule wouldn't get any easier. We didn't seem to have any gimmes on our nonconference schedule. We had just played GIT games with Hamilton and Gallatin, now we had regular season contests at Hamilton and at home with Gallatin.

After our overtime win against Hamilton, we were sure they would be looking for some payback when we went into their place to play. Hamilton jumped out to an early lead, as they did in our first meeting. They were playing intense, physical defense that kept us out of rhythm. We stabilized in the second quarter, matching their intense, physical play. At the half, we trailed 27-20.

In our dressing room at the half, Coach Burke told us we needed to get control of the rebounds and keep Hamilton off the offensive glass. He told me I should work harder to get deep post position and not allow pushing and leaning by Hamilton defenders to displace my positioning.

We played much better in the second half. We were patient and efficient on offense, slowly climbing back into the game, just like in our first meeting. I got posted up deeper and got some points for us in the post. We again featured the balanced scoring that made us dangerous. I scored 14 points, Sawyer had 13, and Kaleb added nine.

We also did as Burke had implored us and controlled the rebounding. In the game, I had 11 rebounds, and Sawyer and Kaleb each had eight. Our combined rebounding efforts helped us limit the number of shots Hamilton got.

Our defense in the second half was some of our best of the year. Hamilton scored only four points in the third quarter. After three quarters, Hamilton's lead was down to two. The game was very similar to the first time we played, with any early Hamilton lead, a gradual Gilman comeback, and a physical, low-scoring style. The final quarter was another intense struggle between Hamilton and Gilman. The game was tied at 39 with less than a minute to go.

Hamilton had the ball, so we prepared for a defensive stand. Kaleb stole the ball and took off, looking for a fast break layup to put us ahead. A Hamilton player chased after him. With the defender right behind him, Kaleb tried to hurry the layup. As the layup was in the air above the rim, the Hamilton player jumped from behind and smacked the backboard. The ball didn't go in. Kaleb had missed, but we expected a goaltending call for the smacking of the backboard. The call wasn't made. Coach Burke later said the referee said he didn't call it because he didn't think the Hamilton player intentionally hit the backboard.

Anyway, Hamilton had the ball again. Again we dug in on defense and got the ball back. With less than 10 seconds to go, Heath got a shot from around the free throw line. It didn't go in and none of us could come up with the offensive rebound. After a foul or a timeout, Hamilton inbounded the ball with a second to go. I stole the errant inbounds pass and let fly a desperation toss to break the tie. I missed, and my shot might have been after the buzzer anyway. We again went to overtime with Hamilton, this time tied at 39.

In contrast to our clutch play in our earlier overtime game against Hamilton, we played poorly in this overtime. Our offense was almost nonexistent. We only scored two points in overtime, on a long jump shot I probably had no business making. Kaleb, Sawyer, and Jarett all fouled out late in the contest as the game slipped away. We lost 50-41.

We had played two fun, exciting, overtime games with Hamilton. One was a euphoric win, one a deflating loss. We seemed to be almost equal teams, so it was fun to try to meet the challenge Hamilton offered. If it had been an NBA playoff series, it probably would have gone seven games.

It was still frustrating to lose, especially after playing so well in the second half to tie it up. We were now 2-3, and next was a home game with Gallatin to close out our four-game stretch of playing Hamilton and Gallatin, the top two seeds from the GIT.

The game with Gallatin was our chance for revenge. We had lost a close one at their house, now we had them at our place. We were used to our court. We knew lots of Gilman fans would be there cheering us on. With the elevated seating area, fans seemed to be right on top of the action in our gym. Gilman fans could create lots of noise and cheering, especially under the great arched roof of Gilman's gym. A local sportswriter once called it the "Thunderdome."

It was a big game. A second chance against Gallatin, our chance for redemption. With so much to be gained with a win, we…choked? Collapsed? Pulled a Hindenburg? Any of these were appropriate descriptions. Gallatin came out with way more intensity than us. They were overwhelming our defense with incredible ball movement and shooting. They used a vicious 3-2 halfcourt trap we couldn't seem to get through. We weren't even getting many shots off. Gallatin brought their "A" game, and we were stuck at our "C" or "D" level, if that. Gallatin built a huge first-half lead, and still their coach was yelling for more. When halftime mercifully brought a break in the beatdown, we had scored all of seven first-half points. Gallatin's lead was over 20. We fought on in the second half for a small shred of pride or dignity. As the starters sat on the bench for the final minutes of Gallatin's 59-24 win, we tried to comprehend how we had played so poorly against a team we had nearly beaten less than two weeks ago. The word that was stuck in my mind was "embarrassment." That's the best word to describe the loss.

We fell to 2-4. Sure, the schedule was tough, but the fact was we had lost three in a row. The most depressing thing was how terrible we had played that night. All our other games had been wins or close losses, no matter what team we played. The Gallatin rematch was a disaster, a blow to the confidence. It was a huge deviation from the level we had been playing at.

Next up was a nonconference game at Polo, followed by our conference opener at Pattonsburg. It was time to refocus and move on. Big games and more challenges lay ahead of us.

CHAPTER 12

It started out like any other day. It took me a class or two to get fully awake and functional. Lockers opened and closed. Teachers issued "good mornings" at intervals along the third floor hallway. The background sound was a mix of pencils being sharpened, people getting drinks from the water fountain, and zippers buzzing from coats and book bags. After school would be practice, then an evening to eat, maybe relax a little, then hit the reset button. The daily routine of high school life rolled on.

The nice thing about high school is, at frequent intervals, some mostly irrelevant, yet interesting issue comes up to break up the monotony. On this particular day, it started with an idea. Desiree was graduating a semester early, so this week in December was her last in high school. Someone in our class came up with the idea of signing out of school around lunchtime and going with Dez to eat in Chillicothe. It would be like an early "senior skip day" so Dez could experience this tradition before finishing out at GHS.

Some students in the senior class thought this would be fun and were eager to go. A couple of us had reservations about the plan, however. To me, the idea didn't seem especially fun, and I figured the school administration would likely go crazy and wildly overreact. It was a decent idea, but it was a great example of "that's not the hill to die on." Also, being the calculating guy that I was, I knew

The four seniors at the captains' meeting before the 2005 Homecoming game. Kaleb (31), Heath (41), Sawyer (32), and I (50) represented our team.

it was basketball season and it would be stupid to jeopardize game eligibility over a day trip to Chillicothe. For some strange reason, I thought of the University of Missouri's "Alma Mater" song, that part that says, "With thy watchwords, honor, duty, thy high fame shall last." My responsibility was to be at school, and there wasn't really any reason not to fulfill this responsibility.

I wasn't above missing school. There were a few times I fulfilled my duty as an American and missed school for a Royals baseball game. However, if you were going to miss school at Gilman High, it was best to plan ahead and tell your teachers you wouldn't be there. If you did this, it was still an unexcused absence and you couldn't make up any homework from that day, but there were otherwise no ramifications for missing that day (so long as you didn't get too many unexcused absences). Just deciding to leave and signing out in the middle of the day was asking for trouble, even if it was a fine display of spontaneity.

My decision not to take part in the midday jailbreak put me in the minority in our class. Mr. Williamson, our third-hour English teacher, heard about the grand scheme. We were visiting at the end of class and he found out I wasn't going. He asked me if I had ever heard of some song. I can't remember the name of the song, but I know it had the word "lonely" in the title.

When lunchtime came, five of the seven seniors in our class at the time—Dez, Krystal, Kaleb, Sawyer, and Blade—made their break. They signed out and headed for Chillicothe. The other two seniors, Heath and I, went through the lunch line. As we sat in the cafeteria and ate lunch, we wondered what, if anything, would come of the "early senior skip day."

It turns out they had a nice time. They ate at El Toro's and got free ice cream for Blade by saying it was his birthday. Meanwhile, an upset principal and basketball coach waited back at the school.

When all was said and done, the five seniors who left early spent the next day in "In School Suspension," which means they went to school but spent the day sequestered in a cubicle. The ISS meant the two basketball players who left, Sawyer and Kaleb, couldn't play in that night's game at Polo.

This also meant Heath and I would be the only seniors playing. A very winnable game was now a great challenge. We would have to rely a lot more on young, inexperienced players. Players who rarely played in games would see lots of playing time that night. Fortunately, it was a nonconference game, so we could get some good playing time for the younger kids without risking a conference game.

We faced a shortage of proven scorers and rebounders. Heath and I needed to have great games for us to win. To be honest, the game was a chance for Heath and I to see what it would be like if our careers had taken place in a different setting. There would be fewer players who could score a lot, so we would score more, but we wouldn't be as good a team. The game, which went badly for us, was a great example of how it's a lot more fun to win than to simply score a lot of points for a weaker team.

Playing shorthanded, we struggled. Polo took a 13-5 lead after one quarter as our offense couldn't get started. Polo keyed on me in the post, and I started slowly, like our team. At the half, we trailed 27-12. Some of our younger players showed some potential, but they weren't quite ready to carry such a heavy load for our team.

The second half was better. I guess it couldn't have been very much worse. We got more accustomed to playing in a game with some of our reserve players. Heath and I got going offensively. I had a 17-point, 12-rebound game while Heath had 15 points and six rebounds. We tried to make up for our loss of offense that came from being without two of our starters. Together, Heath and I scored all but four of our team's points. However, with a good portion of our team scoring and rebounding gone, we needed to do even more if we were to beat Polo. We had four good senior players and some nice role players, but we obviously needed all of us to be successful.

We lost 57-36. Since we were losing badly and had had limited offensive success, I decided to shoot a three late in the game. I went out on the perimeter, got the ball, and put up a three. To the dismay of most everyone in the gym, myself included, the shot went in. It was the first three-pointer I had made in a high school game. I shot a handful of threes that season, but I usually stayed in the post where I was needed and was the most effective. We had enough good perimeter shooters, so I usually just shot threes to provide a spark or as a change of pace. It kind of ended up being a sideshow, a rare curiosity whenever I ventured out to the perimeter and put up a three. I made four of the seven threes I shot that season.

Despite this three and two more from Heath, we lost. We were now 2-5 and riding a four-game losing streak into conference play.

Coach Burke said in the paper that despite our loss, he saw "some good things from some of my younger players and our two seniors who stepped up."

The game was similar to an incident our softball team went through on the day before the state boys softball tournament. We had practice right after school, but Kaleb and Sawyer were late. Coach Burke always made players who were late run six laps around the outfield fence. He told Sawyer and Kaleb to run six laps. After running three laps, they informed Coach Burke they thought they shouldn't have to run that much. They said they were done running. This led to a brief, heated exchange of words, followed by Sawyer and Kaleb leaving. Coach Burke talked like they wouldn't play in the state tournament. We only had 10 players before the two left, so we spent the practice preparing to play with eight defenders. I played first base, so it seemed like I would have to try to man the entire first base side of the infield by myself. The next day, Kaleb and Sawyer apologized to the team and were allowed to go with us and play in the state tournament. Burke didn't think it was fair to make the rest of us play with only eight players.

For the basketball game, however, we still had plenty of players to put five on the court. Also, it was a nonconference game, not the state softball tournament, which may have influenced the different decisions. Both incidents were bumps in the road of seasons. We rallied after the softball controversy, placing fourth in the state tournament. We needed to bounce back now in our basketball season. The Polo game was the last of four straight losses before we started conference play.

We opened HDC play at Pattonsburg. Kaleb and Sawyer could play, but they started on the bench. Under the dome, we started a little slowly on offense. I caught the ball once on the perimeter as we worked through our offense. I saw my defender was playing way off me. I didn't actually shrug my shoulders and say "Why not?" but that was my thought process. I squared up and shot another three. It splashed through the net. That shot kind of helped get our offense going. We got on a roll and turned the game into a rout. Kaleb came off the bench and scored 19 points. Heath had another solid game, with nine points, seven rebounds, and seven assists. We were up 31-15 at the half and cruised to a 53-34 win. The losing streak was over and we were 1-0 in HDC play.

Next up was Christmas break, so we had a lot of practices without games. At one kind of tough practice over break, we did a drill where a player and a partner would run the length of the court, taking turns dribbling up the court and shooting a layup. The other player follows the dribbler, rebounds the layup, and takes his turn dribbling and shooting a layup. Everyone goes at once, so we all ran down and back over and over until coach Burke blew the whistle. Now some players had had a little too much at Christmas dinners or hadn't stayed in shape over break, so some players fell out of line and ran to the trash can. This display of poor conditioning in a few players irritated Burke, who had us keep running and running. Players can lose their edge over Christmas break since they don't play in games, which can make for some difficult practices.

This was especially a problem that season, as snow and ice forced the cancellation of school and some games in January. This led to more practices without games as we kept having practice despite the weather. When school was cancelled due to weather, Coach Burke was sure to specify to only come in to practice if we could make it safely. I took my dad's four-wheel drive pickup, so I could get in to Gilman and back for practice without too much trouble. The high practice, low game period did weigh on us, but we had to keep working and waiting for a chance to play.

Fortunately, we got in our game with Albany in early January, so we got that opportunity to play. Because of Christmas break and the bad weather, it was our only game in a one-month period between games with Pattonsburg and Newtown-Harris.

The Albany game was at home, our first chance to make up for losing badly on our home court to Gallatin. We were thrilled to get to play an actual game, something besides scrimmaging against ourselves.

We played well, taking advantage of our opportunity to play. We built a 27-19 lead at the half. The Albany Warriors played hard and hung around in the third, but we put away our GRC foe with what Coach Burke called "our best fourth quarter of the year by far." Kaleb and Sawyer led our offense, both scoring 18 points. I added seven points and pulled down 10 rebounds, a turnaround from my poor rebounding game a year ago against Albany. As a team, we had control of the boards and ran away with the game, winning 55-40. We always talked about putting teams away in the second half, and we did that against Albany. We played a complete game and improved to 4-5 on the year. The big win at home restored some of the community's confidence in our team. What was supposed to be our great senior year looked to be back on track after an early bump in the road.

Next came Homecoming week, with two home games. On Tuesday we played a conference game with Newtown-Harris, and Friday was the Homecoming game, a conference game against North Harrison, our traditional Homecoming rival.

It was a big week at school with the two home games and all the Homecoming festivities. Adding to it all was activity picture day, which for some reason was during Homecoming week and led to students having their yearbook and NHS pictures taken in Homecoming dress-up day costumes.

One day dearly in the week, as we were working on decorating our wall, we learned we had a new student in our class, Hannah Kunkel. Lots of us were dressed up as fairy tale characters or something and raving about crazy ideas for our wall, but Hannah didn't seem too overwhelmed. This would mean we had eight students in our graduating ceremonies. Most classes at Gilman are bigger than this, usually more like 10-15 students. We mostly got along well in our class. There wasn't too much in-class drama. For our Homecoming king and queen candidates that year, we selected Sawyer and Krystal. Or rather we told Sawyer it was his turn and told Krystal that she had to be the candidate yet again since Dez graduated early and Hannah didn't arrive until the middle of Homecoming week.

In the middle of Homecoming week we shifted our focus to Newtown-Harris. We were looking for a third win in a row, a chance to be 2-0 in HDC play, and a chance to even our record at 5-5. Newtown wasn't great that year, but they had some good players and were a dangerous team. They had a very good coach, Tim Cool, who got the most out of his players. They could hang with most HDC teams.

The Newtown game was similar to the Albany game in that we took a halftime lead and put our opponent away with a nice second half. Newtown really hung tough in the first half. We played just well enough to grab a one-point lead heading into halftime.

We dominated the third quarter. It was an example of how well we could play when we all got going and played our best team game. Our defense held Newtown to eight points in that quarter while our offense put up 22 third-quarter points. It was one of those games when most of our offensive options were having good games, which resulted in a scoring onslaught. I had 18 points, Sawyer had 17, Kaleb had 13, and Jarett added eight. Our offense had a lot of players who could win one-on-one matchups. This could be both a good thing and a bad thing, as sometimes this allowed individuals to jump-start our offense, and sometimes it led to one of us trying to do too much with the ball. Overall, our offense that year was one of attacking the hoop and taking chances. Lots of times this offense was successful, but sometimes it broke down.

It was successful against Newtown-Harris. After our excellent third quarter, we played a solid final period to pick up a 66-48 win. It was our third win in a row and it improved our record to 5-5. Also, in our last chance to win the regular season HDC title, we were 2-0 in HDC play.

We faced another HDC opponent, North Harrison, in our Friday-night Homecoming game. Friday was blue-and-white day, so almost everyone wore the school colors. Some students even broke out the face paint. The walls outside the gym were all decorated. Our wall was Pacman eating Shamrocks since the theme was "Game Over." Our senior class spent part of the day coming up with a skit, which resulted in that classic "Gilman City Idol" skit. It was part of the big pep rally at the end of the day. It was a good pep rally, the rah-rah of high school athletics at its best.

After the coaches' speeches, the skits, the games, the cheers, and the elementary parade of decorations, we usually all stood and sang the school's fight song near the end of pep rallies. It's a classic. It has the same tune as the University of Illinois Loyalty Fight Song. We all belted it out at pep rallies.

> We're loyal to you Gilman High
> To you we'll be true Gilman High
> We'll back you to stand
> Against the best in the land
> For we know you've got sand Gilman High
> Rah! Rah! Rah!
>
> We'll follow the ball Gilman High
> Go crashing ahead Gilman High
> Our team's the best protector
> Our team's the best endeavor
> Three cheers for Gilman High
> Rah! Rah! Rah!

The pep rally ended when school ended, so we all went home for that awkward little waiting period before the Homecoming game.

There was the typically large Homecoming crowd, with the extra bleachers set up on the stage across from the regular seating area. There was the usual Homecoming excitement, plus the anticipation of both the girls and boys teams being good. After a few down years, the Lady Hawks were having a very good year, on their way to a 19-8 overall record. My little sister Abbie was playing on the team as a freshman. Our team had started slowly with a tough early schedule and a couple of bad games, but we had won three in a row and were beginning to show our potential. Both the boys and girls teams could go to 3-0 in HDC play with wins.

The girls team started the night right with a big win over the North Harrison Lady Shamrocks. The Lady Shamrocks were rebuilding and had graduated all but one of their primary contributors from the year before, but it was still an impressive performance from the Lady Hawks.

Then our game. We ran out as our fans cheered and "Thunderstruck" boomed over the speakers. We did layups, the star passing drill, the "Amish" shooting drill, and a little half court three-on-three drill. We just shot for the final minutes. Since we almost always played after our girls team or after another game in a tournament, we didn't get a lot of warmup time. We just got about 10 minutes, so we had to make good use of our time.

The last few minutes were spent in the captains' and coaches' meeting. Coach Burke had the four of us seniors serve as captains. After we exchanged handshakes with the captains and coaches of the other team, referee Russell Hildenbrand talked about a few basic rules and some points of emphasis. He went over the difference between legal defense (fingertips touching the offensive player) and illegal hand checking (a flat hand on the offensive player, impeding his progress). There were the general rules said in most captains meetings, such as no Livestrong bracelets or jewelry. The only jewelry I had ever really won was a class ring, so I was okay on this rule. In the ultra-rural HDC, men didn't really wear jewelry. HDC guys had names for men who wore earrings, and they weren't very nice.

A yearbook photograph captured the moment of this meeting. The four of us seniors stand, hands mostly on hips, shoes reflecting on the gym floor. Our last Homecoming game is minutes away, saturated with possibility. The picture takes me back to that moment, frozen in time by the yearbook camera.

The game was a barn-burner, two great northwest Missouri basketball programs battling it out. We again featured our balanced offense with several points coming from multiple players. Sawyer led us with 18 points, and Kaleb and I both scored 14 points. North Harrison also had several capable scorers, getting 15 points from Nathan Craig, 14 from Nathan Lisle, and 13 from Kasey Parkhurst. With both teams featuring three players contributing 13 or more points, it was a fast-paced, exciting game. Neither team could get much of a lead. I kept looking at the scoreboard throughout the game, hoping in vain to see a bigger lead for the home team.

We played man-to-man defense. Our man defense had improved a lot at the end of my junior season and the early part of the senior campaign. We were confident we could play it with success, even against a team with some offensive power like North Harrison.

It was an intense, draining contest. The electric atmosphere of Homecoming built down the stretch as the game remained close. Sawyer played very well late in the game. He hit some huge shots in the fourth quarter, including one to tie the game in the final seconds of regulation. As exhaustive and competitive as the game had been, we had to summon some more energy because the game went into overtime. It was our fourth overtime in our first 11 games of the season.

Overtime was more good basketball, with both teams hitting big shots to grab the pendulum of momentum for a few fleeting seconds.

With less than 30 seconds to go, North Harrison had the ball with the game tied 55-55. Sawyer was guarding Kasey Parkhurst. Parkhurst got the ball and drove toward the hoop. Our help defense was a little slow in coming and wasn't of the high quality the situation demanded. Parkhurst got off a short jumper and made it to put the Shamrocks up by two. We failed to answer in the final frantic seconds, which gave North Harrison a 57-55 overtime win. The Homecoming heartbreaker loss dropped our senior class to 1-2 in Homecoming games. Both of our Homecoming losses were in overtime. After the game, Coach Burke was kind of upset about our poor help defense at the end of the game and that we had missed some free throws when we might have won the game in regulation.

After the game was the king and queen coronation. Sawyer and Krystal were named king and queen. I'm sure it was a great memory for them. Unfortunately, the game, as exciting as it had been, was a memory of disappointment and opportunity lost. The loss dropped us to 5-6.

After all the activity and attention of Homecoming week came another big week, the Gilman City Invitational Tournament. The senior class always ran the concession stand, so when we weren't playing we had to spend the week working in the concession stand. With tournament games, practices, working in the concession stand, and—oh yeah—school, it would be a very busy week.

Based on our success in the Gallatin Invitational Tournament and our recent three-game winning streak, we got the No. 1 seed in the Gilman Tournament. Our first-round opponent was the King City JV team.

The game was a mismatch, as one could expect in a No. 1 seed/ No. 8 seed matchup. After the first quarter, we were up 22-8. At the half, we led 40-11. We actually played a little sloppily, but we had some good moments. Lots of our players made contributions to the win. We cruised to a 63-22 win. It was a great way to start the tournament week. The win put us into the semifinals against Worth County and evened our record at 6-6.

By the Worth County game, we were all getting tired of working of the concession stand. It would all seem worth it that May when we took our senior trip to Florida. Still, it was nice to leave the stand for a while and go play some basketball.

The game with Worth County was a low-scoring, physical struggle. Kaleb and I got into some foul trouble in the first half and had to sit out for a while. Worth County took a 27-21 lead into halftime. We didn't have any more trouble with fouls in the second half, but we stayed just behind WoCo for much of the second half. We weren't playing our best game, but we were doing what we needed to hang around. We weren't having a good offensive night, but with a great defensive effort and by hitting a couple shots at crucial points, we took a lead in the fourth quarter. Worth County battled back and reclaimed the lead. There was great effort in the final minutes as both teams clawed for a berth in the championship game.

With just a few seconds to go, we had the ball, trailing 45-44. As the final frantic seconds melted away, Kaleb put up an 18-foot jumper. Sawyer and I battled for the rebound position. Kaleb's shot missed, but the ball bounced into Sawyer's vicinity. Sawyer leapt up, using every inch of his considerable vertical leap. He clutched the ball with outstretched hands at the apex of his leap. In the very definition of a last gasp, he flipped the ball up to the hoop while still hanging in air. The ball danced on the rim for a few agonizing fractions of a second. The ball bounced on the side of the rim, fractions of an inch determining if we would experience joy or despair. Eyes all over the gym widened. Finally, the ball went in. Sawyer had won the game for us with a tremendous, buzzer-beating tip-in. It was a sublime play in the most critical of moments. The crowd thundered as we celebrated and the final score lit up the scoreboard: Gilman City 46, Worth County 45. Somehow, we had pulled out the win.

For the fourth year in a row, the Gilman City Hawks were in the final of the Gilman City Tournament. It was also the fifth tournament in a row that we had reached the final in. Our opponent was Ridgeway after their comeback win over Princeton, capped by a buzzer-beating shot of their own. If we could win, it would give Gilman City three championships of the last four years of the tournament.

The season in general was looking up at that point. We were 7-6 and had won five of our last six games. However, since our next game was the championship of a tournament, it received stand-alone significance beyond its role in the context of our season. We wanted a repeat of our great win over Ridgeway in the tournament championship the year before. We wanted to again experience the feeling of being tournament champions.

Another subplot in the championship game, one that wasn't talked about a lot but was still something I sure noticed, was our poor record in tournament championship games. Now I know it's a notable achievement to get the two wins needed to reach the finals and the teams faced in tournament championship games are always very good, obviously. However, the painful truth was that we were 1-4 in tournament championship games. Sure, our last three title game losses were to outstanding teams—North Mercer twice and Gallatin on their home court—but the 1-4 mark was still dismal. This game was our chance to do something about it, to reverse an unsavory trend of battling to the brink before stumbling on the final step.

Regrettably, the dream of reversing that trend was crushed fairly early in our game. After our tough win in the semis we never really got it going in the final.

In a local paper, Coach Burke said, "We didn't bounce back well from the previous game and we looked flat all night."

Maybe we had a letdown game after pulling out the draining win over Worth County. Both Ridgeway and Gilman City had good teams that year, but they played very well and we played very poorly on that night.

Ridgeway jumped out to an early lead. We weren't playing up to their level in the game, but with effort and determination we hung around for a while. Ridgeway had a lead, but we stayed within striking distance until the last few minutes of the half. It was then that the dam broke and our defense finally buckled against the strong offensive challenge Ridgeway presented. Ridgeway outscored us 19-7 in the second quarter to take a 37-17 halftime lead, making our chances of winning our tournament for the second straight year very remote. We grimly battled on in second half, actually outscoring the Owls in the second half but never really threatening to make a real comeback. We lost 64-47. Kaleb had 17 points and I added 10 points, but our offense had stretches where none of us scored much, which was frustrating with all our proven scorers. Overall, it was a very good effort by Ridgeway and a sloppy performance for us.

The loss dropped us to 7-7 on the year. We seemed like we were a lot better than a .500 team, but there we were. We seniors were now an unsightly 1-5 in tournament championship games. We had achieved a lot in playing in six tournament finals, but we seemed to have left a lot of successes and accomplishments on the table, frustratingly close, yet just beyond our reach. Despite our 2nd place finish, we hadn't played real well during the tournament. We defeated a junior varsity squad, used a great tip-in at the buzzer to cover our struggles with Worth County, and played a bad game in the final.

Of course, losing the last game of the week made us look back on the tournament in a somewhat negative light. We had won two of our three games and taken the 2nd place trophy. One point of pride for Kaleb, Sawyer, Heath, and I was that we had made the Gilman City Tournament championship game all three years we played high school basketball, winning once.

After the busy tournament week of playing, practicing, and working the concession stand, it was kind of nice to get back to the normal high school routine. It took me a class or two to get fully awake and functional. Lockers opened and closed. Teachers issued "good mornings" at regular intervals along the third floor hallway. The background sound was a mix of pencils being sharpened, people getting drinks from the water fountain, and zippers buzzing from coats and book bags. After school would be practice, then an evening to eat, maybe relax a little, then hit the reset button. The daily routine of high school life rolled on.

CHAPTER 13

A t its core, basketball is a simple game. A team's ultimate and only real goal is to put the ball in the hoop and keep the other team from doing the same. The basic rules and scoring are wonderfully simple. Tim Wilson, Kaleb's dad, said a few times our game plan needed to be to score more points than we gave up. It was kind of a joke and kind of a commentary on how simple basketball's objective is.

Football has its system of first downs and scoring by kicking or moving the ball across the line. Baseball and softball have ball-strike counts, bases to work around, and then runs. If you ever want to frustrate yourself, try to explain the tennis scoring system to someone who has never watched the game. In contrast, basketball just has baskets—free throws, regular field goals, and threes.

One ultimate goal, two hoops at opposite ends of the hardwood playing surface, and 10 players. It's here that the simple core of the game ends and the controlled chaos begins. There are players and the ball flying all over the court, the crowd making noise and providing the game atmosphere, perfectly executed plays, improvisation, and so many split-second decisions.

This was all on display in our next game, at home against Grundy R-V. Both teams ran up and down the court, trying to out-score the other. Both teams had plenty of capable scorers, which led to a breathless offensive shootout.

As often happened that season, our offense walked a thin line between being a run-and-gun, quick-strike, high-scoring offense and an offense in which individuals tried to create too much. With multiple players who could score, there was temptation for us to do too much as individual offensive players, putting up decent shots when we could maybe get better shots with an extra pass of two. But our quick shooting, attack-from-everywhere approach did result in a lot of points, usually. We had a dangerous offense, one that was surely entertaining to watch.

The problem against Grundy was our defense. Our first half defense was absolutely terrible. We played man defense, but it didn't work. Grundy's Kyle Larson, a sophomore, had a great offensive game. Our guy assigned to him had some trouble guarding him, and our help defense, so critical in man-to-man, didn't get there in time. We let Larson run up too many points and Grundy scored an outrageous 47 points against us in the first half. As the Panthers' points piled up, each of their baskets was met with agitated sighs from the Gilman fans to go with the cheers from Grundy's fans.

Halftime finally came to the rescue with Grundy up 47-34. Coach Burke focused on fixing our defense during the halftime break. Barring a meeting in the conference tournament, this was our last chance to beat the Grundy R-V Panthers. It was rally time, a position we had found ourselves in way too much that season.

We kept firing away in the second half, producing another good scoring half. With only one way to go, our defense improved. We by no means shut down the Panthers, but we slowed them down. Little by little, we chipped away at the big lead Grundy had built. I had an advantage in the post and scored 22 points in the game, including several as we climbed back into the game. In what would be his last game against the coach he once stuck his tongue out at, Les Jackson, Kaleb scored 16 points. Jarett and Sawyer both added double-digit points to the effort.

Despite our improvements in the second half, we had simply dug too deep of a hole. We did manage to cut the Panther lead to single digits late in the game. Unfortunately, Grundy hit enough free throws down the stretch, basketball's classic way to kill a rally. Behind Larson's 29 points, Grundy won 78-69. Three years, three games, three losses to Grundy R-V behind great individual performances by three different players—Andy Peterson, Brad Rains, and now Kyle Larson.

The loss left us at 7-8 on the season. What was meant to be a great, memorable senior season was in danger of becoming a disaster. We had to have a winning record, or forever remember our careers as ending with failure and disappointment. Nobody wanted that.

We could even our record before the HDC Tournament with a game at home against Trenton later that week. It was another match-up with a Grundy County school, this time with Trenton, the bigger, county seat school.

Trenton was an independent school, not in any conference. The school was probably too big for the GRC and yet too small to join the Midland Empire Conference, the conference of nearby Chillicothe. Trenton had a great football tradition. When we didn't have softball games in the fall, my friends and I sometimes went to watch Trenton play at C.F. Russell Stadium. Though we didn't have football at Gilman, I enjoyed going to area towns, watching high school football games, and thinking the teams should pass more. Trenton was a great place to watch a high school football game. Also, Trenton was similar to so many northwest Missouri high schools in that its mascot was a bulldog and its fight song was "On, Wisconsin."

We hadn't played Trenton before, but from what we had heard they were a decent team. We scheduled the game with Trenton because our girls were playing at North Daviess, which didn't have a boys team. We played Trenton in Gilman. With the Lady

Hawks playing at North Daviess, we enjoyed a much longer warm-up period. We arrived early and got to do some extra shooting before the game.

The extra shooting must have helped. We had a 22-10 lead after the first quarter. It was a very good quarter. Our defense redeemed itself somewhat and we got up and down the court very effectively, leading to lots of fast break points.

After the great start, we played fairly even for the rest of the game. We pulled away a little more, but that great start was the key in our 68-50 win. It was another fine offensive game for us. Kaleb had a great all-around game, with 29 points, six rebounds, and five assists. I had an efficient, active post game, with 20 points, 14 rebounds, and four assists. Heath directed our attack with his ball handling, eight points, and four assists. We had a lot of assists as a team in that game. It was an encouraging sign to see us playing well and as an efficient team.

The only drawback that night came when Sawyer, in characteristic pell-mell style, went flying out of bounds after a play. He cut himself badly around his elbow when he hit the metal bar running around the outside of our gym. It was a rather impressive cut. Fortunately, we had a sizeable lead, so we didn't need him to help us mop up the rest of the game. He went somewhere to get it checked out. It wasn't real serious and he didn't miss any games, but the cut did produce its share of blood.

We were now 8-8 as we prepared for the HDC Tournament, hosted by Grundy R-V that year. It was our last chance to win the conference tourney. We had a great chance to win it. Our girls team, fresh off a dominating win over North Daviess, also had a shot at winning the girls title.

We got the No. 3 seed. Our first round opponent was Newtown-Harris. Newtown was a mid-level HDC team that year. Although we beat them by 18 earlier in the year, Newtown had the ability to pull the upset if we weren't careful. If definitely wasn't like a No. 1 seed against a No. 16 seed in the NCAA Tournament. Newtown had a very good coach, Tim Cool, and a good mix of guards and post players. In the years following my graduation, a new wave of players would come up for Newtown-Harris and dominate the HDC. Some of them were on the team my senior year as freshmen and sophomores.

We started our tournament week with a win over Newtown-Harris. We won 55-41 with a good mix of efficient offense and continued improvement on defense. I had a good offensive night, scoring 15 points. It was a nice start to the tournament. Our solid team effort put us in the semifinals against No. 2 seeded Winston.

It was the third year in a row we would play Winston in the HDC Tournament. We played Winston earlier that season, winning in overtime in the Gallatin Tournament. Our games with the Redbirds were almost always close, physical, intense contests. This one, unfortunately, wasn't that close.

An early sign that the evening wouldn't go so great for us came when our warm-up music was played. For some reason, the people at Grundy in charge of such things played Shania Twain's "Man, I Feel Like a Woman." Now there's nothing wrong with Shania Twain, but that might be a song to save for before a girls game. Of course, the song didn't make us play bad, but it did lead to some sophomoric giggles.

The game itself was bad from the start. Winston seized the early lead as we experienced offensive struggles. After the first quarter, Winston led 18-10. We continued to struggle to get points in the second quarter. Coach Burke was unhappy with the officiating and got a technical in the first half. He might have partially been trying to fire us up because we had played so poorly early in the game.

After starting the tournament with a good game, I had a very off night against Winston. We were fighting for a spot in the HDC

Tournament championship game, desperately needing points, and I couldn't seem to hit anything. It was very frustrating. I thought I made a nice play to hit a layup in transition but was called for traveling. It seemed to be one of those nights. Some nights just seem to be off nights and no amount of effort will make things go right. It's like some situations in life; I guess you just have to keep pressing on. I kept working and finished with eight points, but our team needed a better, more efficient game from me.

We trailed by 15 at the half. Our offense finally got going in the second half, largely because Kaleb started burying some shots. He hit four threes and had 25 points in the game. The problem was Winston kept pouring in points to keep us at bay. The Redbirds had four players score 14 or more points, so they always had someone to hit a shot whenever we tried to crawl back into the game. We just couldn't make the play or shot at a critical point to get us back in the game. Winston won by double digits. Like the Grundy R-V game, it was a reminder that we couldn't give a good team a double-digit halftime lead and expect to win.

For us seniors, the dream of winning an HDC Tournament was crushed. In lieu of achieving that goal, we had a chance to beat North Mercer and win the 3rd place game. It was also the third time in a row we would play North Mercer in the HDC Tournament. Mercer and Grundy R-V were the only HDC schools our senior class had never beaten, and this was our chance to take Mercer off that list. It was also our first meeting with Mercer since losing to them in overtime in the District championship game. This was our chance for revenge. Heath, Kaleb, Sawyer, and I were 0-6 against Mercer. That had to stop. We're not gonna take it anymore. No, it wasn't the HDC Tournament championship, but this was a huge game.

Our girls team was in the girls championship game, playing—you guessed it—North Mercer. It was a Gilman City-North Mercer doubleheader, first the boys 3rd place game, then the girls championship.

Our game was at 5:00 p.m. Saturday, so we all loaded onto the bus that afternoon and headed for Galt. We could all sense this was a big night. Coach Burke had prepared a scouting report on North Mercer. They were still a top-tier HDC team, but they were a little different than the team we played three times the year before. They had a new coach, Nathan Heinrichs, after Dan Owens decided to just be North Mercer's superintendent. Some of their key players, such as Girdner and Holmes, had graduated, while a new wave of talented young players, such as Austin Hague and Ben Stark, had taken lead roles on the team. Also, there were some players back from the year before to provide leadership, such as senior Levi Hague.

Coach Burke had printed copies of the scouting report, which had analysis of North Mercer by "Coach X" and "Coach Y." It was helpful to see what coaches who had faced Mercer that year thought. It also got us in the mindset of what we needed to do to beat Mercer.

It was a very close game, as expected. Nothing was easy against Mercer. After a disappointing performance against Winston, I bounced back with a nice game in the post, scoring 17 points against the Cardinals. Heath and Kaleb's outside shooting complimented my interior game, as well as Sawyer's midrange shots and drives to the hoop. At times during the season our attack sputtered when only one of us could score consistently. In the game against North Mercer, our offense was efficient and balanced. We scored in a variety of ways.

Despite our quality play, Mercer stayed right with us. Neither team could gain any sizeable advantage. In all games, especially trophy games, the intensity builds as games stay close late into the game. There wasn't any down time, any time to catch your breath in this game. It was a deep, exhausting struggle throughout. Big shots were followed by bigger shots as the fickle momentum swung back and forth as rapidly and repeatedly as a kid on a swing during recess.

The challenge of trying to finally beat North Mercer got a little harder for me at the end of the first quarter. I grabbed a defensive rebound with about a second left in the quarter and went to throw it toward our hoop at the other end of the court. Mercer's Austin Hague alertly tried to knock the ball out of my hands. He either bumped me or smacked the ball or a little of both. This happened just as I was about to throw the ball at our hoop like a quarterback, so I lost my balance and fell. All of my 185 pounds landed on my right knee. Coach Burke wanted a foul to be called, maybe get some free throws for me, but the refs didn't think there had been a foul. In any event, I hit my knee pretty hard and it was sore. I didn't tell anyone and kept on playing. I tried to run as normal as I could, but I knew I probably ran with a slight limp. I didn't want Mercer players to know my knee hurt some and I didn't want Coach Burke to know because he might have taken me out for a while. Besides, it wasn't an excruciating injury and we had a chance to beat Mercer and win the 3rd place trophy. I had to play on and not let my level of play slip at all.

The only problem was when I quit running at halftime my knee got a little stiff. It loosened up some as I played and ran in the second half.

We were all so determined to overcome and finally beat North Mercer. We got a lead of just a couple points in the fourth quarter and grimly hung on. Late in the game, I was posted up on the low block. The player defending me was trying to keep me from getting posted up very deep. I dug in, trying to stay low and keep my feet set wide. I couldn't let myself be moved. The Mercer player then tried to push me off the block with his arms. He pushed me hard enough my jersey came untucked and a foul was called. We were in the bonus, so I had free throws. As I walked to the line, tucking in my jersey, Coach Burke said, "We need these." Naturally, Coach. I made just over 70% of my free throws that year, but it's always hard to stand still and have a good shooting stroke when you have been running and jumping so much. I took a breath and made both free throws, finding comfort in the splash of the net. Our tiny lead grew by two.

Our defense held on down the stretch, trying to keep Mercer at bay. However, with a few seconds to go, Mercer was down three and had the ball. Our defense dug in for one more stand. Levi Hague's contested, NBA-range three at the buzzer fell short, and we had finally defeated North Mercer. Gilman City 52, Mercer 49.

We took pictures with our 3rd place trophy. It wasn't the champion's trophy, but it was still a nice way for us seniors to end our HDC Tournament careers. After the thrill of victory, now it was time to cheer on the Lady Hawks in their tournament championship game.

We normally played after our girls team, so we couldn't watch all of their games. We had to get dressed and prepared during the fourth quarter of their games. Fresh off our win over North Mercer, we could fully focus on cheering the Lady Hawks on in their game with the Lady Cardinals. We were very vocal, supportive fans. Kaleb and I both had little sisters on the team. It was another close, intense game. In the end, our girls pulled out a win. It was a breakthrough win, announcing the arrival of the Lady Hawks in the upper echelon of the HDC.

The sweep of North Mercer in the back-to-back trophy games was a memorable night. Aside from the Lady Hawks winning their tournament, we had finally defeated North Mercer and our senior class had won our last HDC Tournament game. The sense of achievement, the thrill of victory, going through an intense and exhaustive struggle and coming out on top—these were the great post game feelings that Saturday night. It was the positive result of being "the man in the arena." At the best, he knows, in the end, the triumph of high achievement.

The win over Mercer was our eighth in our last 12 games. Our record improved to 10-9. We were gaining momentum as our season, the last season, barreled on toward its conclusion.

The 2004-05 Gilman City Hawks pose for a photo after beating North Mercer for third in the HDC Tournament. Front row from left: Daniel Dennert, Steven Braden, Sawyer DeWitt, Heath Oram, Kaleb Wilson, Matt Eason, and Jonathan Elder. Back row from left: Black Johnson, Kyle King, Zach Harris, Jarett Webb, Benjamin Herrold, Daniel Miles, and Coach Brent Burke.

CHAPTER 14

With two traditionally lower-tier teams, North Daviess and Cainsville, unable to field teams during the 2004-05 season, the HDC was a very challenging conference to play in. Except for our game at Pattonsburg, just about every game was difficult. There were not many easy victories on the schedule. The overall quality of play was high that year. Any time you take the two worst teams out of a league, it gets harder to be successful in that league. We didn't have any easy wins to pad our HDC record.

With only nine HDC schools fielding teams, we had eight HDC conference games. The snow and ice of early January had also changed our HDC schedule. Our game at Tri-County was moved to late February, the last week of our regular season. Because of this, we had four HDC games before our conference tournament and four games after it.

We were 2-2 in HDC play heading into the week following the conference tournament. We felt we were much better than a .500, mid-pack HDC team, but we had lost two HDC games at home, to North Harrison in overtime and to Grundy R-V by nine. We could have contended for the HDC crown, but we really hurt our chances with our inconsistent play against those beatable-but-dangerous teams so common in the HDC that year.

Our lapses into mediocrity during our final season were frustrating. Remember this was one of the things I was known for, my place in Gilman City society. I was a sports guy who cared a lot about basketball and was a good player. Not succeeding in one of the main things I hung my hat on was irritating. This was senior year, our time to succeed.

Even though our early losses made our chances of winning the HDC regular season title remote, we had a chance to show we could play with the HDC's best in the week after the conference tournament. We played at North Mercer and at Ridgeway, two of the HDC's top teams.

First came the rematch with Mercer. Our narrow win over the Cardinals showed how even we were. Now we were playing in a gym North Mercer was obviously used to, which made playing them more of a challenge. Mercer had a nice gym, though, so I felt comfortable playing there. Playing in the HDC conditions you to adapt to different courts, with the variety of square and fan backboards and the different court sizes and surfaces.

Perhaps since we had played each other a few days before, the game started with a slower, deliberate pace and not much scoring. We played well early on, taking a 10-7 lead after one quarter.

Both offenses inevitably started scoring more in the second. Both teams had multiple scoring threats, and good scorers usually find ways to do their thing. As expected, the game stayed close. Mercer grabbed a slim 24-22 halftime lead, setting the stage for a great second half to settle things.

We came out and started the second half with a great stretch of basketball. We kept Mercer's scorers in check and hit enough shots to regain the lead. That year our senior players seemed to take turns having good scoring nights. That night Sawyer and I both had double-doubles. I had 20 points and 11 rebounds while Sawyer scored 17 points and pulled down 10 rebounds. All those rebounds gave us control of the boards, which helped us grab a 36-32 lead going into the last quarter. After losing six in a row to North Mercer, we were on the brink of back-to-back wins against them. We needed to put the game away.

With both teams desperately trying to win, the fourth quarter was a wild shootout. We had a good offensive attack in the fourth quarter, but we couldn't seem to keep up with Mercer. After scoring 32 points in the game's first 24 minutes, the Cardinals exploded for 28 points in the final eight minutes.

The Hague brothers led Mercer's scoring outburst. Senior Levi Hague had 21 points (including three three-pointers) and sophomore Austin Hague had 18 points. Mercer's scoring was a mighty wave we couldn't stop. They simply outscored us. Our maddening defensive breakdowns, reminiscent of our first half meltdown against Grundy R-V, only enabled Mercer's offensive onslaught to continue. Heath West hit four three-pointers for the Cardinals, some of which came at key points down the stretch, what Bill Raftery would call "daggers."

In the end, we failed to put the game away and were simply outgunned by the Cardinals. North Mercer won, 60-53. Our record fell to 10-10, including an unsightly 2-3 in HDC play.

We had to shake off the disappointing blown save of a loss and focus on our next game, at conference leader Ridgeway.

The Ridgeway Owls were having a memorable year. They would have some good seasons in the following years, but the 2004-05 season stands out. Sometimes sports teams just have a year that stands out, achieving almost mythical status. Saying "1985" to Royals fans or "1986" to Mets fans brings up magical memories. Sometimes there is a year when it all comes together and a season separates itself from all the others for a team, like Illinois' nearly unbeaten 2004-05 season. Ridgeway was 20-2 coming into the game with us. They had won 13 games in a row and were state-ranked for the first time in a long time. This night was a big night for them, both Homecoming and Senior Night. They were looking to clinch the HDC title that night as well. It was their turn in the spotlight.

It was our chance, our duty, to try to ruin it all. We were a veteran team. We had played in big games before and we had defeated some very good teams already that year, such as Hamilton, Winston, and North Mercer. We knew the players on the Ridgeway team very well. Our teams had been largely the same as we played each other several times in our junior high and then high school days. We had played some good games, so we knew this would probably be another good game between us. Even with our bad loss to the Owls in the Gilman City Tournament championship, our team had won four of our six high school games with Ridgeway heading into that night's matchup.

In practice prior to the game, Coach Burke gave us a brief warning. He said he had heard some bad stories about the referees at Ridgeway, saying they were two guys he had never seen officiate before. He told us to focus on playing and let him worry about the referees. At the game, there were two referees I had never seen before, but I think they did an okay job. I never liked to blame the refs for losing, or even really the other team's performance. I tried to give credit to other teams when the played well, but I felt we almost always won or lost based on how we played. I thought the responsibility of winning and losing was ours, based on how we played.

We were out on the court warming up when "Black Betty" came blaring over the speakers and the Owls came running out to the cheers of their fans. I stayed focused on getting ready to play. We were the spoiler, the underdog, even the villain to all those Ridgeway fans. No matter who won, that team would have to earn this one.

It was a close game. Ridgeway didn't run off to a big early lead like in our last meeting. With great effort, the Owls took a small first half lead. Aaron Fitzpatrick led the Owls on offense that game, as he did in most of their games that year. His 17 points led the Owls' scoring. Ridgeway also benefited from 14 points from senior Dylan Hogan. Mark Kyle Wilson also had double-digit points. Like us, the Owls had a variety of capable scorers. By halftime, Ridgeway had pulled out a 34-26 lead. Once again, we had given a good team a halftime lead, making for quite a hill to climb in the second half.

In the second half, we started to chip away at Ridgeway's lead. Our offense was balanced, which was when it was most dangerous. Four players scored double-digit point totals. Kaleb had 13 points, Sawyer had 12, and I had 11. Sophomore Kyle King hit several big jumpers for us as he scored 10 points. Our defense tightened, as it did from time to time, and we slowly reeled in Ridgeway. We started to get the momentum. I hit a layup and got fouled to further cut Ridgeway's lead. I've got your Black Betty right here. We were on the brink of an upset.

Unfortunately, we didn't get any further than the brink. After again falling behind to a good team at the half, our dramatic rally attempt again fell just short. Ridgeway held on for a 58-53 victory. They definitely earned it. The victory had seemed within our grasp, but we just couldn't quite pull it off. Our frustration was familiar; it was our seventh loss by nine points or less that year.

We were now 10-11 overall and 2-4 in HDC play. Against top-tier HDC competition, we had lost three of our last four games. We had one more week, three more games, before Districts. Two of the games were HDC games. We had a week to straighten things out before Districts.

The Sunday at the start of this week was FFA Sunday. We all dressed up in our stiff FFA jackets and black pants and went to the First Baptist Church of Gilman City. I normally went to the Blue Ridge Christian Union Church, but FFA Sunday was at Gilman City Baptist, so I went there.

Tim Wilson, Kaleb's dad, was the preacher at Gilman City Baptist. I always enjoy hearing him preach. He tells it like it is, speaking with such passion and enthusiasm for God's Word. On FFA Sunday, he preached from Romans 12, a powerful chapter. He spoke on verses 14-16. They read:

Bless those who persecute you; bless and do not curse. Rejoice with those who rejoice; mourn with those who mourn. Live in harmony with one another. Do not be proud, but be willing to associate with people of low position. Do not be conceited.

These verses really had an impact on me. They talk about acting like a Christian should even when it is difficult or seems to go against human nature. It's powerful stuff. I left the service feeling energized. This was good, because a busy, eventful week lay ahead.

I had never thought about scoring 1,000 points in my basketball career when I first started out as a sophomore. The idea did cross my mind when Jeff Girdner and Brad Rains scored their 1,000th points while playing us. When I rode up with Jacob Wilson to the 2003 District championships in Eagleville, after my sophomore season had just ended, we talked about it a little. Scoring 1,000 points, although impossible without the help of teammates, seemed like an individual goal in a team sport. I was kind of uncomfortable talking about it the few times I did. It's easy to talk about now that I'm done playing, but it wasn't then.

Still, it's pretty cool to score over 1,000 points. That is a lot of satisfying swishes of the net, especially since I scored those points with almost no help from the 3-point line. My scoring came from setting up close to the hoop, attacking the rim, grabbing offensive rebounds, running hard on fast breaks, and looking for open spaces on the court. To be honest, the idea of scoring 1,000 points crossed my mind a few times that year, although I don't think it was a distraction for me.

After the Ridgeway game, I had scored 989 points, 11 shy of 1,000. Our next game was Monday night at Tri-County, our biggest rival.

Besides the 1,000 point issue that was somewhere in the back of my mind, this game was big because it was likely my senior class' last game against Tri-County. The Mustangs were not in our District, so, barring a meeting in the state playoffs, this was our last chance to beat them. We had won three straight against our biggest rival, and it would be great to end our basketball careers with a winning streak against the Mustangs intact.

Normally we dressed in a classroom at Tri-County, but this time they had our team changing in a small bathroom down a hall, around a corner, and down another hall from the gym. It was kind of crowded and there wasn't any place to sit even if one of us had wanted to.

After unloading our stuff in our cramped little "locker room," we went to the gym to watch our girls team play.

For some reason, not all the lights were working in Tri-County's gym. It was light enough to see and play, but it was kind of dim. The players on the court looked like a moving version of a faded, poorly lit photograph. It was kind of strange, but we played on. As we watched our girls win their game, word got around that I was close to 1,000 points. I think my brother, Seth, said something about it as he was talking to me before our game. Soon enough it was time for us to get ready for our game. It was nice to be able to simply focus on playing basketball.

We grabbed the early lead against the Mustangs. We created a lot of turnovers by pressing them, getting some points in transition and keeping the Mustangs from running their offense. We were up 33-18 at halftime. Some players asked me at the half if I had 1,000 points yet. I said I would get them soon enough as we played and let's just focus on this game. It was kind of awkward to be asked about it during the game. I felt like it was a little distracting.

I had scored 10 points in the first half, so I knew I would eventually get the one more point I needed just as we played our game. I always liked beating Tri-County, so I really wanted to win big in our last game against the Mustangs. Beating the Mustangs was a nice diversion from everybody asking me questions.

In the second half, I hit a layup, going over 1,000 points for my career. The Mustangs did make a run at us in the third quarter, but we locked down defensively and stopped their rally. We had a very good defensive half. Backup center Zack Harris and I had a lot of blocks. He was about 6'4", like me, and was a good shot blocker. I got enough blocks to almost have a triple-double, finishing with 12 points, 14 rebounds, and a career-high nine blocks. On a night that people talked about the points I scored, it was my rebounds and blocks that were above average.

Jarett and Kaleb hit a lot of shots in the second half as we cruised to one more win over Tri-County. They both had 13 points. We won our fourth in a row over Tri-County, 58-37.

After the game, I talked for a little bit with Bruce Sweet, a Tri-County player who went to the same church I did. He was just a sophomore, but he was already a very good player. I noticed he had a bloody lip, so I asked how that happened. In a good-natured way, he informed me I had accidentally given him the bloody lip when we made contact sometime during the game.

After the game, some people congratulated me. The Bethany Republican-Clipper account of the game mentioned I had scored my 1,000th career point in the game. After the game, Dad arranged to get the game ball for me to keep. He had to buy a basketball from Gilman City and trade it for the 1,000-point ball, which was the property of Tri-County.

That dim night in the gym was another memorable one. Reaching the 1,000-point milestone brought on those feelings of having achieved something and having earned that honor. I listed scoring over 1,000 points in basketball as one of my greatest high school achievements in our graduation program that May. I also listed being Valedictorian.

I rode home with my parents after the game. Since it was out of the way to go back through Gilman on our way home, I left my pickup at the school. I think I left the keys in the ashtray, but there's a chance I forgot to do this and left the keys in the ignition. Either way, it probably wasn't a smart decision to leave my pickup in town overnight. I caught a ride into town the next morning with Dad. I walked by my pickup.

I could tell things on the inside of the vehicle had been moved around. The outside of the vehicle seemed a little muddier than before. I heard early in the day what had happened. Kaleb, Sawyer, and some of the younger high school kids had stolen my pickup and used it and another pickup to make donuts in the school's yard.

Because of the way word travels around Gilman and the sources I had, I soon knew what Sawyer and Kaleb had done. It was annoying that these two people I thought were my friends had done this.

I wasn't sure if it was just supposed to be a joke or not. I don't know if they were jealous that I had scored 1,000 points and they had not. It's pointless to try to figure their reasoning; they were likely drunk, even though it was a Monday night.

The thing was, I knew they did it before they knew I knew. I heard people ask Kaleb and Sawyer if they knew what happened and they lied time and time again. I asked Kaleb if he knew what happened and he told me he didn't know. Those lying little cowards, I thought, why don't they talk honestly with me about it all? I didn't ever get really angry. After all, my pickup was just fine. I was more disappointed. It was "mankind's essential illness" on display yet again.

Fortunately, God used the event to teach and refine me. Ironically, I recalled the verses Kaleb's dad, Tim, had preached about on FFA Sunday. "Bless those who persecute you, bless and do not curse." I had to act like a Christian towards Kaleb and Sawyer, regardless of what they did. I didn't always achieve this, being by all accounts far from perfect, but my attitude toward them had to be to "bless and do not curse." It was hard to do this and go against human nature, but God's work in people's lives is rarely easy. He gave me opportunities to do this. A few weeks after this all happened, Mizzou hosted an NIT game. My brother and I invited Kaleb to go with us and he rode down with us. It was a fun time, even though Mizzou got torched by Drake Deiner and DePaul.

The issue was over for me. I let the school worry about its felony vandalism investigation. Sawyer did say he was sorry one night as we talked on senior trip, which was nice.

As it always did regardless of what happened off the court, the basketball season rolled on. Next was senior night against Winston, my last home game ever. They announced all of us seniors, listing our high school activities, basketball accomplishments, and future plans. Blade did the announcing. He mentioned I had just scored my 1,000th point the night before.

Before our game, a Winston player who had heard this jokingly bragged about scoring his 100th career point. It was kind of funny. Referee Alan Berry also wished us good luck in our future plans and said he had enjoyed refereeing our games and watching us play.

It was the ninth and final time our senior class would play Winston. Winston had some seniors that year who had played against us in all those games. With our career series tied at four games apiece, it was the ultimate rubber match. After so many close games with Winston, we would have one more.

Winston took the early lead. The Redbirds were up by seven after the first quarter. We slowly reeled them in in the second quarter, but we couldn't quite catch them. Our offense wasn't playing well in the first half. Winston led 27-25 at the half. The third quarter was a stalemate. We entered our last quarter ever at the Gilman City gym trailing by two. We were in real danger of going out with a loss. Senior Night, always a mix of emotions, might have been more bitter than sweet.

Fortunately, we responded with one last rally for the home crowd. Kaleb and Sawyer hit some big shots down the stretch on their way to double-digit point totals. After struggling offensively for much of the game, I hit a couple of big buckets as we rallied past the Redbirds. Heath added nine points while directing our offense. The four of us seniors dug in one last time at home. One more time we scrambled around the court, hustling to make plays for old Gilman High. We went "crashing ahead," as our fight song says. One more time we defended our home court and won. We ground out a 55-52 win, allowing our last memory of playing on our court to be walking off it as winners.

The win improved our record to 12-11. Our final conference record was 4-4, kind of mediocre. We had one more nonconference game before Districts, at Osborn. Like our game at Osborn my sophomore year, it snowed on our trip down.

We had a little trouble early on with our man defense, but we used a little zone and got points in transition to pull away. I bounced back from a below average offensive night against Winston to score 20 points against Osborn. I had a size and experience advantage in the post, and my teammates gave me opportunities with good post entry passes. We cruised to a 66-43 win.

It was our third win in a row, all of which came the week before Districts. The win improved our record to 13-11. Things were looking up for our team at just the right time. For the final time, my senior class of players headed into Districts, looking to achieve the elusive goal of winning the thing.

CHAPTER 15

Good men, the last wave by, crying how bright
Their frail deeds might have danced in a green bay,
Rage, rage against the dying of the light.
— *Dylan Thomas*

The District Tournament, always intense and emotional, is different for seniors. A loss means the death of a senior's career. Nearly every team has seniors, so almost every District game ends someone's basketball career. "Play like it's your last game" becomes more than just another motivational saying; it becomes an omnipresent reality.

A District game with careers on the line is a great show. Seniors (with the help of the underclassmen, obviously) frantically try to extend their careers. They are not quite ready to let go, usually, not quite ready to quit playing. Even when I was on the court, the idea crossed my mind that if we didn't win I was done playing. Players battle to the very end, their competitive spirits still burning bright, not wanting to give up the highest level of sports competition most of them will ever know. When scoreboards with their harsh reality show insurmountable deficits and dwindling time, everyone in the gym realizes the end is coming. Tears come to the eyes of mothers and even some fathers because they are just so proud.

Often, seniors are removed late when the games are in hand, so they get one last great ovation from their fans. This is a very emotional moment as players walk off the court for the last time, wearing the sweat-drenched uniforms of their schools for the last time. This walk-off ovation is one last salute to the hometown heroes. It is one last moment in the spotlight for the players.

Seniors usually have the desire to play on, but a loss at Districts means their high school basketball careers are over, ready or not. They are like the Confederate soldiers after General Lee surrendered, who didn't want to give up and asked for one last chance to beat the Yankees. A loss in Districts is a forced surrender for a basketball player.

Of course, life goes on with or without basketball. It is still fun to play basketball for as long as you can. The District Tournament ends a lot of careers, but some team has to win it. That team will have memories of a District title and an appearance in the state playoffs at the end of their careers.

After coming so very close to winning a District title my junior year, my senior class had one last chance to win Districts. Our first-round opponent was the Newtown-Harris Tigers. We had beaten Newtown twice earlier in the season, although they had hung around in those games. A good game by us should result in a win, but it wouldn't be an easy win.

We got our good game, starting with a dominating first quarter. Our offense was on that night, scoring 20 or more points in each of the first three quarters. Our defense kept the Tigers from getting many quality shots to get going early in the game. We had a 20-7 lead after the first quarter. Behind our offense, we slowly pulled away after taking the early lead. We were up 43-20 at the half. This would not be our last game. Newtown got some late points to trim our final margin of victory, but we held control of the game throughout the second half. Basketball is really fun when you are playing well and things are working.

Near the end of the third quarter, we had the ball and a sizeable lead. With about 20 or 30 seconds left in the quarter, Coach Burke wanted us to run down the clock and take one shot just before the buzzer. I went out on the left wing as we ran through our motion offense. I heard Coach call out "One shot!" but I caught the ball on the wing and realized I was open. I squared up from beyond the arc and let fly a three just before my defender could get there. It splashed through the net, the fourth and final made three of my season and my career. I was glad it went in or else Coach might have been a little upset. He sometimes called for one shot with 30 seconds or less in a quarter, but he didn't mind us shooting earlier than the final few seconds if we could get a quality shot.

Despite some increased scoring by Newtown very late in the game, we won, 76-63. Like every year I played, we moved out of the first round and into the District semifinals.

We looked good in our first-round game. Four of us scored 13 or more points in the game, led by Sawyer's 17. Kaleb had 16, Jarett had 14, and I had 13. When several of us were making shots, we could really rack up the points. The win, which improved our record to 14-11, put us in a semifinal matchup with the North Mercer Cardinals.

For the third year in a row, we faced the North Mercer Cardinals in Districts. In our two previous meetings, Mercer had ended our seasons en route to winning District titles. It was our senior class' ninth overall meeting with Mercer. We had an unsightly 1-7 record against them heading into our District semifinal showdown. During my career, Mercer had been a buzzsaw during Districts, but after our breakthrough toppling of the Cardinals in the HDC Tournament we felt ready to turn the tables in the March (Districts) portion of our rivalry.

Before our game was the other District semifinal. Ridgeway narrowly defeated Worth County, 41-37, to advance to the District championship game. Then it was our turn to take the stage.

For the 80th consecutive time, I put on the Gilman City high school uniform. I carefully tucked in the top, lining up the stripes on the sides that would get hopelessly askew during the game. For the 80th consecutive time, I pulled on my shoes and laced them up. I stretched and jumped up and down a little, loosening my muscles for another great effort. Coach Burke gave instruction and we broke our huddle. For the 80th consecutive time, I ran out onto the court with my team to the cheering of the Gilman fans and then was announced as a starter.

We played decently early on. We played a steady, efficient, team game early on. Mercer hung with us. We scratched out a one-point lead after the opening quarter. It felt like another battle for District survival with North Mercer was upon us.

We stumbled a little in the second quarter. It began to feel like one of those "lost in the fog" nights. We began to play sluggish, listless defense. This was disastrous when combined with Mercer's explosive offense that year. I played my part in our team's sudden malaise. I didn't play very well in the second quarter. It slowly turned into one of those nights when no amount of effort or focus could make things work for me. One time, Kaleb had the ball in transition and I had gotten up the court, behind the Mercer players. Kaleb threw the ball up the court to me. If I could have handled the pass, I would have had a layup. The pass was above my head, but I still should have caught it. I put my hands up but the ball somehow slipped through them and out of bounds. I was in disbelief. My career was on the line, and my hands were failing me.

We pressed on. I kept working and hustling, finding ways to get something going in the post. At the half, Mercer led 29-25. It was only a four-point deficit. Our season and some of our careers hung in the balance, but the telling chapters of the game were yet to be written.

We came out in the third quarter with a furious offensive attack aimed at catching the Cardinals. Kaleb and I led the offensive surge that night. He had 11 points that night and I had 10. These point totals gave us a boost, but they were below our season averages. Still, our offense scored 15 points in the second quarter, a great total for getting back into the game. Unfortunately, we couldn't turn off the faucet of Mercer's offense. Mercer counted our offensive improvement by putting up 18 points that quarter. Mercer's lead stretched to seven after the third quarter. The fog we seemed to be playing in thickened. The light of our careers faded.

In the fourth, the Cardinals kept pouring it on. We couldn't guard Austin Hague in our man defense. He scored 27 points for Mercer, beating back our rallies with big shots. Mercer had yet another great offensive quarter, scoring 19 points in the final quarter. Our defense just kept breaking down. We needed a tourniquet to stop the scoring.

We scored some, but we couldn't keep up. As the final quarter wore on, the light faded some more. It became more and more unlikely we would win. My career seemed to be nearing its end. The only thing left for us to do was rage, rage against the dying of the light. We furiously battled on, fighting on against the mounting odds and growing darkness.

Late in the game, I got the ball in the lane, elevated, and banked in one more shot. It was the final field goal of my high school career, the last two of my 1,051 career points.

We fouled some to try to extend the game late, but Mercer was out of reach. On one play, Mercer's Ben Stark, a post player, had briefly tried to dribble up the court before passing to a teammate. The teammate was fouled. As we lined up for free throws, Austin Hague told Stark not to try to dribble up the court since he was a post player, not a ball-handling guard. I looked at the two younger post players and said, "They never let me dribble either."

Coach Burke took me out of the game in the waning seconds so I could get one last ovation from the crowd. For the last time, I walked off the court, proudly wearing my Gilman City jersey. Mercer won, 66-51. For us seniors, our high school careers were over.

North Mercer went on to beat Ridgeway in the District Championship game. Mercer eliminated us and won the District every year I played. They lost in the sectional playoff game at Chillicothe.

We finished the year 14-12. We technically also had two forfeit wins, over North Daviess and Cainsville, but I didn't count them toward our record because these schools didn't field teams or even start the season. I included the forfeit win over North Daviess on my junior year team's record because North Daviess started the season but could no longer field a team when it was our turn to play them. Since North Daviess was a part of some HDC teams' schedules my junior year, I included our forfeit win over them on our final record.

Our 14-12 mark was about on par with our 15-13 record the year before. To be brutally honest, however, my final season was a little disappointing. We wanted to have a great senior season, but our record was barely above .500. We wanted to win the HDC title, but we were a mid-pack team in the standings. We also failed to reach the finals of the HDC Tournament or Districts. We had reached both the year before. We didn't win any of our four tournaments during my senior season. There was a feeling of unmet potential, almost anticlimax when we were supposed to be having a special final year. There were players who admitted they really didn't have fun playing that year. We seemed to play a little tight and a little as individuals at times, and this cost us.

Of course, there were good moments, like finally beating Mercer or knocking off No. 1 seeded Hamilton in overtime to advance to the GIT final. Sure there was pressure, but I had a lot of fun playing that year. It was fun to be the unflappable veteran, to be a team leader, to give it my all in competition playing a game I love.

I was again named First Team HDC All-Conference. I averaged 13.3 points per game on 50% shooting. I also made 70% of my free throws. I also averaged 9.2 rebounds and 2.7 blocks per game.

For my three-year, 80-game career, I had 1,051 points, 683 rebounds, and 158 blocks. We went 37-43 in those 80 games. With our one forfeit win, my senior class had a 38-43 career record. We were a pretty successful team after starting our careers 2-10.

Kaleb was a unanimous selection to the HDC All-Conference First Team. He averaged 14.6 points, 4.9 rebounds, and 2.7 assists per game. Sawyer added 10.3 points and 5.3 rebounds per game and was named HDC All-Conference Honorable Mention. Heath had directed our offensive attack with 5.9 points and 3.9 assists per game.

All of us seniors now had to move on. After my last game, some people in the community told me now I could get on with real life and the rest of my life.

I considered playing college basketball. I had some contact with a few Christian colleges about their basketball teams. I also thought about playing basketball at Division III Cornell College in Iowa. I talked with some of Cornell's coaches on the phone and had some correspondence by mail with them. I felt confident I could play college ball and thought it would be fun to keep playing. However, I ended up going to the University of Missouri in Columbia to major in Journalism. I got some good scholarships and I liked MU. I wanted to be a sportswriter and MU has a great journalism school. I made the transition to cheering sports fan and rec league/pickup game player. I still love playing and watching sports.

I ride my bike a lot. It filled some of the competitive void left by high school basketball. It is a different kind of competition, me against those unforgiving hills and, sometimes, the stopwatch. Sometimes I ride at an easier pace, just enjoying the ride or thinking about stuff.

Basketball is still a big part of my life. I go crazy at Mizzou basketball games and spend huge amounts of time in March watching the NCAA Tournament. I play 21 and H-O-R-S-E with my friends at college. We formed a rec league basketball team, but we didn't do very well. I also go up to my church's gym and play basketball with my friends and family. I really enjoy playing basketball with my friends, or even just shooting by myself, listening to the bouncing ball and the swish of the net.

My three years playing high school basketball for Gilman City were full of great memories, achievements, and disappointments. Sometimes watching games takes me back to those memories. Sometimes when I am shooting for fun I will take a shot from a certain spot on the court and think back to shots I took in games from the same areas. I remember countless hours spent trying to improve, shooting and running and working through drills. I loved playing basketball and striving to be my best for old Gilman High. It was a cultural thing, a part of who I am and a link to my community. It was a blessing to be able to be a part of it and experience playing high school basketball for Gilman City. Looking back, my high school hoops career was a great three-year adventure, a cultural, social, educational, and recreational experience. Life goes on and greater things than basketball have happened and will happen, but I will always enjoy my memories of playing high school basketball, those three years when I was a ballplayer for Gilman High.